Reef Aquariums Husbandry:
A Beginner's Guide

Understanding Water Parameters, Feeding and Nutrition, Maintenance and Care, Advanced Filtration Methods, Troubleshooting Issues and Breeding Marine Fish.

Louis Shepherd

Table of Contents

Introduction

Welcome to the mesmerizing world of reef aquariums! Whether you're a curious beginner or a seasoned hobbyist looking to expand your knowledge, this book is your gateway to unlocking the secrets of underwater ecosystems.

In "Reef Aquariums Husbandry: A Beginner's Guide" we embark on a journey to discover the beauty and complexity of reef aquariums. These miniature oceanic realms, teeming with vibrant corals, fascinating fish, and captivating invertebrates, offer a glimpse into the wonders of the marine world.

But where do you begin? Fear not, for this book is your trusted companion on your reefkeeping adventure. We'll start by unraveling the basics: what exactly is a reef aquarium, and why might you be drawn to this enchanting hobby? From there, we'll delve into the essential considerations for planning and setting up your own reef tank, guiding you through the selection of equipment, the intricacies of water chemistry, and the art of creating a thriving aquatic environment.

As you embark on this journey, you'll discover the joys and challenges of caring for a living reef. From selecting the perfect combination of corals and fish to maintaining optimal water quality and managing potential issues, we'll equip you with the knowledge and skills you need to succeed as a reef aquarist.

But reefkeeping is not just about creating a beautiful display—it's also an opportunity to connect with nature, to learn about the delicate balance of marine ecosystems, and to contribute to conservation efforts. Throughout this book, we'll emphasize the importance of responsible reefkeeping practices and offer insights into how you can make a positive impact on coral reef conservation.

Whether you're dreaming of transforming a corner of your home into a slice of the ocean or simply seeking to deepen your appreciation for the marine world, "Reef Aquariums Husbandry" is your comprehensive guide to creating and maintaining a thriving underwater oasis. So, dive in, explore, and let the wonders of the reef captivate your imagination!

Chapter 1

Understanding Reef Aquariums

Imagine yourself immersed in the tranquil depths of a coral reef, surrounded by a kaleidoscope of colors and life. The gentle sway of corals, the graceful dance of fish, and marine creatures create a symphony of beauty and wonder. This is the enchanting world of reef aquariums—a gateway to the mysteries of the ocean, right within the confines of your own home.

In this chapter, you embark on a journey of discovery as we unravel the essence of reef aquariums. What exactly defines a reef aquarium, and what sets it apart from other forms of aquatic habitats? What draws enthusiasts from all walks of life to the allure of these miniature underwater worlds? As we delve deeper, we'll uncover the captivating features that make reef aquariums a fascinating and rewarding hobby.

Join us as we peer beneath the surface and explore the enchanting realm of reef aquariums, where every coral colony tells a story, and every fish is a vibrant character in the ever-unfolding narrative of life beneath the waves. Prepare to be captivated, inspired, and transported to a world where the boundaries between imagination and reality blur, and the wonders of the ocean come alive before your eyes.

What is a Reef Aquarium?

Reef aquariums, often referred to as coral reef aquariums or simply reef tanks, are specialized marine aquarium setups designed to replicate the complex and diverse ecosystems found in natural coral reefs. These captivating underwater environments are home to an astonishing array of life, including corals, fish, invertebrates, and microorganisms, all living in harmony within a delicate balance.

Components of a Reef Aquarium

A reef aquarium typically consists of several key components:

1. Aquarium Tank: The foundation of the reef system, the aquarium tank provides a controlled environment for marine life to thrive. Tanks come in various shapes and sizes, ranging from small desktop setups to large custom-built displays.

2. Live Rock: Live rock is a porous calcium carbonate material harvested from natural coral reefs or aqua cultured. It serves as both a decorative element and a biological filter, providing surface area for beneficial bacteria to

colonize and aiding in the breakdown of organic waste.

3. Substrate: The substrate, typically made of sand or crushed coral, covers the bottom of the tank and provides a habitat for beneficial microorganisms and detritus-eating organisms like snails and hermit crabs.

4. Filtration System: Reef aquariums employ various filtration methods to maintain water quality. This may include mechanical filtration to remove debris, chemical filtration to absorb impurities, and biological filtration to break down organic waste.

5. Lighting: Proper lighting is essential for the health and growth of photosynthetic organisms, such as corals and algae, in the reef aquarium. LED lighting systems are commonly used due to their energy efficiency and customizable settings.

6. Circulation: Adequate water circulation is crucial for oxygenation, nutrient distribution, and waste removal within the aquarium. Powerheads and wave makers are often used to create turbulent water flow, mimicking the natural currents found in coral reef environments.

Principles of Reef Aquarium Ecology

Reef aquariums function as self-contained ecosystems, governed by the same ecological principles that govern natural coral reefs. Understanding these principles is essential for creating and maintaining a healthy reef aquarium:

- Biodiversity: Coral reefs are among the most biodiverse ecosystems on the planet, hosting a multitude of species that rely on each other for survival. Similarly, a diverse array of corals, fish, and invertebrates contributes to the stability and resilience of a reef aquarium.

- Symbiosis: Symbiotic relationships are prevalent in reef ecosystems, where organisms form mutually beneficial partnerships. For example, corals host symbiotic algae called zooxanthellae, which provide them with essential nutrients through photosynthesis.

- Nutrient Cycling: Like natural reefs, reef aquariums rely on efficient nutrient cycling to maintain water quality. This involves the biological breakdown of organic waste into less harmful compounds by beneficial bacteria and other microorganisms.

- Stability and Balance: Stability and balance are key principles of reef aquarium ecology.

Fluctuations in water parameters, such as temperature, salinity, and pH, can stress or harm aquarium inhabitants. Maintaining stable environmental conditions is essential for the health and longevity of the reef ecosystem.

Benefits of Keeping a Reef Aquarium

Aesthetic Beauty and Tranquility

Reef aquariums are like living works of art, with arrays of colors provided by vibrant corals, exotic fish, and dazzling invertebrates. From the fluorescent hues of LPS (Large Polyp Stony) corals to the iridescent shimmer of schooling fish, the visual spectacle of a well-maintained reef aquarium is unparalleled.

Watching the gentle sway of corals in the current and the graceful movements of fish can transport you to a serene underwater world. The soothing ambiance of a reef aquarium can provide a peaceful retreat from the stresses of everyday life, offering moments of relaxation and reflection. Unlike static decorations, the inhabitants of a reef aquarium are dynamic and ever-changing. As corals grow and fish interact, the aquarium evolves into a living masterpiece, captivating viewers with its natural beauty and dynamic energy.

Educational Opportunities and Discovery

Reef aquariums offer a unique opportunity for hands-on learning about marine life and ecosystems. As hobbyists care for their aquariums, they gain insights into the biology, behavior, and ecology of reef organisms, fostering a deeper appreciation for the natural world. With a reef aquarium, you can observe the behaviors and interactions of marine life up close, from the symbiotic relationship between corals and algae to the territorial disputes among fish. Each day brings new discoveries and insights into the fascinating world beneath the waves.

By learning about the delicate balance of coral reef ecosystems and the threats they face, reef aquarium enthusiasts can become advocates for marine conservation. Through education and outreach, they can raise awareness about the importance of protecting coral reefs and inspire others to take action.

Therapeutic Value and Well-Being

Studies have shown that spending time with aquariums can reduce stress and anxiety levels, promoting a sense of calm and well-being. The rhythmic movements of fish and the gentle sway of corals have a soothing effect on the mind and body, helping to alleviate tension and promote relaxation. Caring for a reef aquarium provides mental stimulation and a sense of purpose, as hobbyists engage in tasks such as feeding, maintenance, and observing aquarium inhabitants. The challenges and rewards of reef keeping stimulate the mind and foster a sense of accomplishment.

In our increasingly urbanized world, reef aquariums offer a direct connection to the natural world, bringing a slice of the ocean into our homes. By nurturing a miniature coral reef ecosystem, we can reconnect with nature and develop a deeper appreciation for the beauty and complexity of marine life.

Social Engagement and Community

Reef aquarium keeping is a hobby that fosters a sense of community and camaraderie among enthusiasts. Whether through online forums, local clubs, or aquarium expos, reef keepers come together to share knowledge, experiences, and advice, forming friendships that transcend geographic boundaries. Reef aquarium enthusiasts have the opportunity to share their passion with others through educational outreach and public engagement. By hosting aquarium tours, giving presentations, or participating in reef conservation initiatives, they can inspire others to appreciate and protect coral reef ecosystems.

For many reef keepers, the ultimate reward is passing on their knowledge and passion for reef aquariums to future generations. By instilling a love for marine life and conservation in children and grandchildren, they ensure that the benefits of reef keeping endure for years to come.

In conclusion, the benefits of keeping a reef aquarium extend far beyond mere aesthetics. From the educational opportunities and therapeutic value to the social engagement and environmental awareness it fosters, reef keeping offers a rich and rewarding experience that enriches both the mind and the soul.

Chapter 2

Planning Your Reef Aquarium

Embarking on the journey of setting up a reef aquarium is an exciting and rewarding endeavor. However, like any significant project, proper planning is essential to ensure success and avoid common pitfalls along the way. In this chapter, we will guide you through the process of planning your reef aquarium, from setting clear goals and choosing the right tank size to selecting essential equipment and establishing a realistic budget. Whether you're a beginner taking your first steps into the world of reef keeping or an experienced hobbyist looking to refine your approach, careful planning is the foundation upon which a thriving reef ecosystem is built. So, let's dive in and begin the exciting journey of bringing your reef aquarium vision to life.

Setting Goals for Your Aquarium

Setting clear and achievable goals is the first step in planning a successful reef aquarium. By defining your objectives and priorities, you can tailor your aquarium setup to meet your specific needs and preferences. In this section, we'll get to know the importance of setting goals for your reef aquarium and provide guidance on how to identify and prioritize your objectives.

Understanding the Purpose of Your Aquarium

For many hobbyists, the primary goal of a reef aquarium is personal enjoyment and relaxation. Creating a visually stunning underwater landscape filled with colorful corals and fish can provide hours of fascination and enjoyment, serving as a source of tranquility and beauty in your home. Reef aquariums offer valuable educational opportunities, allowing hobbyists to learn about marine life, ecosystems, and conservation. If your goal is to deepen your understanding of marine biology and ecology, you may choose to focus on maintaining a diverse and healthy ecosystem that closely mimics natural coral reefs.

Some hobbyists may be interested in breeding marine fish or propagating corals as a way to contribute to conservation efforts and preserve endangered species.

By setting up a reef aquarium with breeding in mind, you can create a sustainable ecosystem that supports the reproduction and growth of marine life.

Identifying Key Objectives

One of the first decisions to make when setting goals for your reef aquarium is determining the size of the tank. Consider factors such as available space in your home, budget constraints, and the level of commitment you're willing to make to maintenance and care. Another important consideration is the type of marine life you wish to keep in your aquarium. Are you primarily interested in keeping fish, corals, or a combination of both? Do you have specific species in mind that you'd like to include in your reef ecosystem?

The layout and design of your aquarium, known as aquascaping, can have a significant impact on its visual appeal and functionality. Consider whether you prefer a naturalistic reefscape with rocky outcroppings and caves or a more minimalist design with open swimming space and artistic arrangements of corals.

Prioritizing Your Goals

When setting goals for your reef aquarium, it's important to distinguish between essential requirements and optional enhancements. Identify the core elements that are non-negotiable for achieving your desired outcome, such as adequate lighting for coral growth or a reliable filtration system for water quality.

Budgetary constraints can also influence your goals and priorities for the aquarium. Determine how much you're willing to invest in equipment, livestock, and ongoing maintenance, and allocate your resources accordingly. Keep in mind that certain goals may require a higher initial investment but can lead to long-term savings or benefits.

Consider your timeline for setting up and maintaining the aquarium, as well as your long-term vision for its growth and development. Are you looking to create a fully matured reef ecosystem from the outset, or are you willing to take a gradual approach and allow the aquarium to evolve over time?

Review and Refinement

Setting goals for your reef aquarium is not a one-time process but an ongoing journey of review and refinement. Periodically revisit your objectives to assess your progress and make adjustments as needed based on changing circumstances, new insights, or lessons learned from experience. Don't hesitate to seek advice and inspiration from experienced reef keepers, aquarium forums, and online resources. Learning from the experiences of others can provide valuable insights and help you refine your goals and strategies for success. Finally, remain flexible and adaptable in your approach to goal setting. Unexpected challenges or opportunities may arise along the way, requiring you to adjust your plans and priorities accordingly. Embrace the journey of discovery and enjoy the process of bringing your reef aquarium vision to life.

By setting clear and achievable goals for your reef aquarium, you lay the groundwork for a rewarding and fulfilling experience that brings you joy, learning, and a deeper connection to the fascinating world of marine life. So take the time to define your objectives, prioritize your goals, and embark on the journey of creating your own slice of the ocean in your home.

Choosing the Right Tank Size and Location

Selecting the appropriate tank size and location is a critical decision that sets the foundation for your reef aquarium. In this section, we'll see factors to consider when determining the size of your tank and finding the optimal location within your home.

Tank Size Considerations

Begin by assessing the available space in your home where you intend to place the aquarium. Measure the dimensions of the area, taking into account any furniture, doors, windows, or other obstructions that may impact the placement of the tank. Consider the dimensions of the tank in relation to the available space. While larger tanks offer more room for creativity and stocking options, they also require more floor space and can be heavier and more challenging to maintain. Smaller tanks are more compact but may have limited stocking options and require more frequent maintenance.

The size of the tank directly impacts its water volume, which in turn affects water stability and the ability to maintain optimal water parameters. Larger tanks tend to have more stable water conditions and dilute waste more effectively, while smaller tanks may experience greater fluctuations in temperature, pH, and nutrient levels.

24

Location Considerations

Ensure that the chosen location can support the weight of the aquarium, stand, and equipment. Avoid placing the tank near structural weaknesses, such as load-bearing walls, or on uneven surfaces that may cause instability. Consider the ease of access to the tank for maintenance tasks such as water changes, feeding, and cleaning. Choose a location that allows ample space around the tank for maneuvering and accessing equipment.

Be mindful of natural light and sunlight exposure in the chosen location. Direct sunlight can lead to excessive algae growth and temperature fluctuations, while indirect sunlight may affect the viewing experience and contribute to algae issues.

Ensure that the chosen location has access to electrical outlets for powering equipment such as lights, heaters, and pumps. Consider the placement of plumbing connections for water changes and filtration systems, as well as the proximity to drains and water sources.

Tank Size Recommendations

Common tank sizes for reef aquariums range from small nano tanks (under 20 gallons) to large custom-built displays (over 100 gallons). The ideal size for your tank depends on your goals, budget, and available space.

While smaller tanks can be appealing for their compactness and affordability, they also present challenges in terms of water stability and stocking options. As a general guideline, a minimum tank size of 30 gallons is recommended for beginners to provide a more forgiving environment and greater stocking flexibility. If space and budget allow, consider scaling up to a larger tank to provide more room for creativity and experimentation. Larger tanks offer greater stability, dilution of waste, and opportunities for aquascaping, stocking, and coral growth.

Location Optimization Tips

Choose a location away from high-traffic areas to minimize disturbances and stress on aquarium inhabitants. Avoid placing the tank near doors, walkways, or areas frequented by pets or children. Select a location with stable temperature and environmental conditions to minimize fluctuations that can stress aquarium inhabitants. Avoid placing the tank near drafty windows, heaters, air conditioners, or heating vents.

Consider the aesthetic impact of the tank location on the overall ambiance of the room. Choose a location that enhances the visual appeal of the aquarium and complements the existing décor and furnishings.

By carefully considering the size and location of your reef aquarium, you can create an optimal environment that promotes the health and vitality of your aquatic ecosystem. Take the time to assess your available space, structural considerations, and environmental factors to ensure a successful and enjoyable reef keeping experience.

Essential Equipment and Supplies

Equipping your reef aquarium with the right tools and supplies is essential for creating a thriving and balanced ecosystem. In this section, we'll take a look at the key equipment and supplies you'll need to set up and maintain your reef aquarium, from the tank itself to essential accessories like lighting, filtration, heating, circulation, and testing kits.

Aquarium

Choose a tank size that accommodates the needs of your aquatic inhabitants and fits within the available space in your home. Common materials for aquarium tanks include glass and acrylic, each with its own advantages and considerations in terms of clarity, durability, and weight.

Invest in a sturdy and level aquarium stand that can support the weight of the tank and provide a stable foundation. Consider the material, design, and aesthetics of the stand, as well as any additional features such as storage space or built-in compartments for equipment. Depending on the species of fish and other inhabitants in your aquarium, you may need a lid or cover to prevent them from jumping out of the tank. Choose a lid or cover that allows for adequate ventilation and light penetration while providing security and protection for your aquatic pets.

Lighting

Selecting the right lighting system is crucial for supporting the growth and health of photosynthetic organisms such as corals and algae. LED (Light Emitting Diode) lighting is a popular choice for reef aquariums due to its energy efficiency, customizable spectrum, and long lifespan. Other options include T5 fluorescent, metal halide, and hybrid lighting systems. Establish a lighting schedule that mimics the natural day-night cycle and provides sufficient light intensity and duration for photosynthesis. Gradually acclimate corals and other light-sensitive organisms to new lighting conditions to prevent stress or bleaching.

Invest in a lighting controller or timer to automate your lighting schedule and ensure consistency and stability. Programmable controllers allow you to adjust the intensity, color spectrum, and duration of light cycles to meet the specific needs of your aquarium inhabitants.

Filtration

Biological filtration is essential for breaking down organic waste and maintaining water quality in the aquarium. Utilize live rock, porous ceramic media, and other biological filter media to provide surface area for beneficial bacteria to colonize and convert harmful ammonia and nitrite into less toxic nitrate.

Another type of filtration, Mechanical filtration helps remove debris and particulate matter from the water column, preventing it from accumulating and fouling the aquarium. Use filter socks, filter pads, or micron filter media to trap solid waste and improve water clarity.

Finally, Chemical filtration involves the use of specialized media such as activated carbon, phosphate remover, and nitrate absorbers to remove dissolved impurities and contaminants from the water. Incorporate chemical filtration as needed to address specific water quality issues or maintain optimal conditions for sensitive organisms.

Heating

Maintaining a stable water temperature is crucial for the health and well-being of your aquarium inhabitants, especially tropical species that require warm water conditions. Use a reliable aquarium heater with built-in thermostat controls to regulate water temperature within the desired range. Position the heater(s) in an area of the aquarium with good water circulation and away from direct contact with substrate or decorations to prevent overheating or damage. Distribute multiple heaters evenly throughout the tank to ensure uniform heating and minimize temperature fluctuations.

Consider investing in a backup heater or temperature controller to provide redundancy and peace of mind in case of equipment failure or power outages. A backup heater can help maintain stable temperatures and prevent thermal shock to sensitive organisms during emergencies.

Circulation

Adequate water circulation is essential for oxygenation, nutrient distribution, and waste removal within the aquarium. Use powerheads, wavemakers, or circulation pumps to create turbulent water flow and simulate natural currents found in coral reef environments. Experiment with different flow patterns and placement of circulation devices to achieve optimal water movement and distribution throughout the tank. Aim for a combination of direct flow and random flow to prevent dead spots and ensure thorough filtration and nutrient export. Choose circulation devices with adjustable flow rates and flow patterns to tailor water movement to the specific needs of your aquarium inhabitants. Periodically adjust flow settings to prevent debris buildup, promote coral health, and encourage natural behavior in fish.

Testing Kits

Regular testing of water parameters is essential for monitoring the health and stability of your reef aquarium. Invest in high-quality testing kits for parameters such as temperature, salinity, pH, ammonia, nitrite, nitrate, alkalinity, calcium, and magnesium. Develop a regular testing schedule to monitor key water parameters and detect any deviations from optimal levels. Test water parameters at least once a week, or more frequently during the initial setup phase, after significant changes, or in response to observed issues or abnormalities.

Also, familiarize yourself with the recommended ranges and ideal values for each water parameter based on the specific requirements of your aquarium inhabitants. Use test results to identify potential problems, make informed adjustments to your aquarium setup, and maintain a healthy and balanced environment for your aquatic pets.

In Conclusion, by equipping your reef aquarium with the essential equipment and supplies outlined in this section, you lay the foundation for a successful and thriving aquatic ecosystem. From the tank itself to lighting, filtration, heating, circulation, and testing kits, each component plays a crucial role in supporting the health and vitality of your aquarium inhabitants. So invest in quality equipment, establish a reliable maintenance routine, and enjoy the beauty and tranquility of your reef aquarium for years to come.

Budgeting for Your Reef Aquarium

Creating and maintaining a reef aquarium can be a rewarding hobby, but it's important to plan and budget carefully to ensure that you stay within your financial means. In this section, we'll familiarize ourselves with the various expenses associated with setting up and maintaining a reef aquarium, as well as tips for budgeting effectively and maximizing the value of your investment.

Initial Setup Costs

The cost of the aquarium and stand is one of the most significant expenses when setting up a reef aquarium. Prices vary depending on the size, material, and brand, so research different options and choose one that fits your budget and aesthetic preferences.

Factor in the cost of essential equipment and supplies such as lighting, filtration, heating, circulation, and testing kits. Invest in quality equipment that meets the needs of your aquarium inhabitants while staying within your budget. Consider the cost of purchasing fish, corals, invertebrates, live rock, substrate, and other decorations to populate your reef aquarium. Prices vary depending on the species and quantity, so prioritize your purchases based on your budget and stocking preferences.

Ongoing Maintenance Costs

Budget for ongoing expenses such as electricity, water, and possibly salt mix for water changes. Keep in mind that certain equipment, such as lighting and filtration, may increase your utility bills, so factor these costs into your budget accordingly. Plan for the cost of replacement parts, filter media, additives, and other consumable supplies needed for routine maintenance and upkeep. Stock up on essentials like filter pads, activated carbon, and test reagents to avoid unexpected expenses.

Also, budget for the cost of feeding your aquarium inhabitants, including fish food, coral supplements, and invertebrate feeders. Research the dietary requirements of your livestock and choose high-quality foods that provide essential nutrients and promote health and vitality.

Budgeting Tips and Strategies

- Set a Realistic Budget: Determine your budget for the initial setup and ongoing maintenance of your reef aquarium based on your financial situation and priorities. Be realistic about what you can afford and avoid overspending by sticking to your budget.

- Prioritize Essential Expenses: Identify the essential expenses that are necessary for the health and well-being of your aquarium inhabitants, such as equipment, supplies, and livestock. Allocate the majority of your budget to these priority items and prioritize quality over quantity.

- Research and Compare Prices: Shop around and compare prices from different suppliers to find the best deals on equipment, supplies, and livestock. Take advantage of sales, promotions, and discounts to save money on your purchases without compromising on quality.

- DIY and Upcycling: Consider DIY (Do-It-Yourself) projects and upcycling techniques to save money on aquarium equipment and decorations. Repurpose household items or build your own equipment, such as aquarium stands, sumps, or aquascaping tools, using affordable materials and resources.

- Plan for Future Expenses: Anticipate future expenses such as equipment upgrades, additional livestock purchases, and unforeseen emergencies by setting aside a contingency fund or savings buffer. Having a financial safety net in place can help you address unexpected expenses without disrupting your budget.

Maximizing Value and Return on Investment

While it may be tempting to cut costs by purchasing cheap or low-quality equipment, investing in reliable and durable equipment upfront can save you money in the long run. Quality equipment is more efficient, durable, and less likely to malfunction or require frequent repairs or replacements. Adopt sustainable practices such as water conservation, energy efficiency, and waste reduction to minimize ongoing expenses and environmental impact. Choose energy-efficient lighting, practice responsible feeding habits, and implement water-saving techniques to reduce utility costs and promote environmental stewardship.

Approach reef keeping as a long-term investment in your hobby and personal enjoyment. Set realistic goals, establish a sustainable budget, and prioritize ongoing maintenance and care to ensure the long-term health and success of your reef aquarium.

By budgeting wisely and planning strategically, you can create and maintain a beautiful and thriving reef aquarium that brings you joy, relaxation, and a deeper connection to the wonders of the underwater world. So take the time to assess your financial resources, set clear priorities, and invest in the essentials that will help you achieve your reef keeping goals while staying within your budget.

Chapter 3

Creating Your Reef Aquarium

Embarking on the journey of creating your own reef aquarium is an exciting and fulfilling endeavor. In this chapter, we will guide you through the step-by-step process of bringing your aquatic vision to life, from selecting the perfect tank and aquascaping your underwater landscape to introducing your chosen inhabitants and maintaining a healthy ecosystem. Whether you're a novice enthusiast or an experienced aquarist, the creation of your reef aquarium is a journey filled with discovery, creativity, and wonder. So let's dive in and begin the adventure of crafting a vibrant and thriving marine ecosystem that will captivate and inspire for years to come.

Cycling Your Tank

Cycling your tank is one of the most crucial steps in the setup process of a reef aquarium. This process establishes the beneficial bacteria colony necessary to break down harmful ammonia and nitrite into less toxic nitrate, creating a stable and healthy environment for your aquatic inhabitants. In this section, we'll explore the importance of cycling your tank, the methods for achieving a successful cycle, and tips for ensuring a smooth transition for your reef aquarium.

Understanding the Nitrogen Cycle

The nitrogen cycle is a natural biological process that occurs in all aquariums, including reef aquariums. It involves the conversion of ammonia (produced by fish waste and decaying organic matter) into nitrite by beneficial bacteria, followed by the conversion of nitrite into nitrate by a different group of bacteria. Nitrate is then removed from the water through water changes, biological filtration, or chemical filtration.

Beneficial bacteria play a critical role in the nitrogen cycle by breaking down ammonia and nitrite, which are highly toxic to aquatic life, into nitrate, which is less harmful at lower concentrations. Establishing a colony of these bacteria is essential for maintaining water quality and preventing ammonia and nitrite spikes that can stress or harm aquarium inhabitants. The cycling process typically takes several weeks to complete, during which time beneficial bacteria colonize the aquarium surfaces, filter media, and substrate. Cycling may involve fluctuations in ammonia and nitrite levels as the bacterial populations establish and stabilize, so patience and regular monitoring are key.

Methods for Cycling Your Tank

Fishless cycling involves adding a source of ammonia to the aquarium, such as pure ammonia, fish food, or a decaying piece of seafood, to kick-start the nitrogen cycle without exposing fish to harmful levels of ammonia and nitrite. This method is considered more humane and allows for greater control over the cycling process.

Fish-in cycling involves adding hardy fish species to the aquarium to produce ammonia through their waste, kick-starting the nitrogen cycle. While this method can be faster than fishless cycling, it can also be more stressful for the fish and may require frequent water changes to maintain water quality.

Another method for cycling your tank is to seed the aquarium with beneficial bacteria from an established source, such as filter media, substrate, or live rock from an existing tank. This can help accelerate the cycling process by introducing a ready-made colony of bacteria to jump-start the nitrogen cycle.

Tips for a Successful Cycle

1. Monitor Water Parameters: Regularly test the water parameters, including ammonia, nitrite, nitrate, pH, and alkalinity, throughout the cycling process to track the progress and ensure that conditions remain safe for your aquarium inhabitants. Invest in high-quality test kits and follow the recommended testing frequency for accurate results.

2. Perform Partial Water Changes: During the cycling process, it's important to perform partial water changes as needed to dilute any accumulated ammonia or nitrite and maintain water quality within safe limits. Aim for a nitrite level of zero ppm and an ammonia level below 0.25 ppm before adding any sensitive livestock to the tank.

3. Be Patient and Observant: Cycling a tank requires patience and observation as beneficial bacteria populations establish and stabilize. Avoid rushing the process or adding livestock prematurely, as this can lead to stress or harm for your aquarium inhabitants. Instead, take the

time to monitor water parameters and wait for the cycle to complete before introducing any fish or corals.

4. Consider Using Beneficial Supplements: Some hobbyists opt to use beneficial supplements, such as bottled bacterial additives or live bacterial cultures, to accelerate the cycling process or boost bacterial populations in the aquarium. While these products can be helpful, they should be used in conjunction with proper cycling methods and regular testing to ensure effectiveness.

5. Avoid Overfeeding: During the cycling process, avoid overfeeding your aquarium inhabitants, as excess food can lead to an increase in ammonia and nitrite levels. Feed sparingly and remove any uneaten food to prevent organic waste buildup and maintain water quality.

Understanding the importance of cycling your tank, choosing the right method for your setup, and following these tips for a successful cycle, you can establish a stable and healthy environment for your reef aquarium inhabitants to thrive. Remember to be patient, monitor water parameters regularly, and take the time to ensure that conditions are optimal before introducing any fish or corals to your newly cycled tank.

Aquascaping with Live Rock and Substrate

Aquascaping is the art of arranging rocks, substrate, and other decorative elements in your aquarium to create a visually appealing and functional underwater landscape. Live rock and substrate play key roles in providing structure, stability, and habitat for your reef aquarium inhabitants. In this section, we'll delve into the importance of aquascaping, the benefits of using live rock and substrate, and tips for creating a stunning aquascape that enhances the beauty and biodiversity of your reef aquarium.

Understanding Aquascaping

Aquascaping serves both aesthetic and practical purposes in a reef aquarium. It creates a naturalistic environment that mimics the habitats found in the wild, while also providing shelter, hiding places, and territory for aquarium inhabitants. A well-designed aquascape enhances the visual appeal of the tank, promotes natural behavior in fish and corals, and contributes to the overall health and stability of the ecosystem. There are several principles and techniques to consider when aquascaping your reef aquarium, including balance, proportion, focal points, and depth. Balance the layout by distributing visual weight evenly across the tank, use proportion to create harmonious relationships between elements, create focal points to draw the eye and add interest, and create depth by layering rocks, substrate, and decorations.

Aquascaping materials include live rock, substrate, sand, driftwood, and artificial decorations, each of which can be used to create different effects and textures. Live rock and substrate are particularly popular choices for reef aquariums due to their natural appearance, biological filtration benefits, and ability to support coral growth and colonization by beneficial microorganisms.

Benefits of Live Rock

Live rock serves as a natural biological filter in the aquarium, hosting a diverse community of beneficial bacteria, algae, and microorganisms that help break down organic waste and maintain water quality. The porous structure of live rock provides ample surface area for bacterial colonization and nutrient processing, making it an essential component of a healthy reef ecosystem.

Live rock provides habitat and shelter for a variety of aquarium inhabitants, including fish, invertebrates, and corals. Its irregular shapes and crevices create hiding places and territorial boundaries, allowing shy or nocturnal species to feel secure and exhibit natural behaviors. Live rock acts as a substrate for coral growth and colonization, providing a stable foundation for corals to attach and spread. Over time, corals encrust and grow on the surface of live rock, forming intricate structures and contributing to the overall beauty and biodiversity of the reef aquarium.

Choosing and Arranging Live Rock

There are several types of live rock available for aquascaping, including base rock, cured live rock, and aquacultured live rock. Base rock is inert and serves as a foundation for aquascaping, while cured live rock is already colonized by beneficial bacteria and organisms. Aquacultured live rock is sustainably harvested from aquaculture facilities and often comes with a diverse assortment of corals and invertebrates.

When arranging live rock in your aquarium, consider factors such as stability, aesthetics, and functionality. Start by placing larger, heavier rocks at the bottom of the tank to create a stable foundation, then build upwards with smaller rocks to create height, depth, and visual interest. Leave ample space between rocks for water flow and circulation, and avoid stacking rocks too tightly to prevent collapse or instability. There are various aquascaping styles and techniques to choose from, including natural, minimalist, reef crest, and island reef. Each style emphasizes different elements such as rock formations, open space, or coral colonies, allowing you to create a unique and personalized aquascape that reflects your taste and preferences.

Substrate Selection and Placement

Substrate refers to the material placed on the bottom of the aquarium, such as sand, crushed coral, or aragonite. Choose a substrate type that complements your aquascape design and meets the needs of your aquarium inhabitants. Fine sand is ideal for delicate species like sand-sifting fish and bottom-dwelling invertebrates, while coarse substrates may be better suited for high-flow environments. Consider the depth and coverage of the substrate when aquascaping your tank. Aim for a uniform depth of substrate throughout the tank, with thicker layers in areas where burrowing or digging species are present. Avoid creating deep sand beds (DSBs) unless specifically required for certain types of organisms, as they can trap debris and promote anaerobic conditions.

When adding substrate to your aquarium, distribute it evenly across the bottom of the tank and use a leveling tool or your hands to smooth out any uneven areas. Avoid piling substrate too high against the glass walls or stacking it too close to rocks and decorations, as this can impede water flow and create dead spots where detritus accumulates.

Maintenance and Care

Regular maintenance is essential for keeping your aquascape clean and healthy. Use a gravel vacuum or siphon to remove debris and detritus from the substrate during water changes, and gently brush or rinse live rock surfaces to prevent algae buildup and maintain water quality. Avoid disturbing the substrate excessively to prevent clouding and disruption of beneficial bacteria colonies.

Monitor live rock surfaces and substrate for signs of algae growth, such as green or brown diatoms, hair algae, or cyanobacteria. Address algae issues promptly by adjusting lighting, nutrient levels, and water flow, and consider adding algae-eating livestock such as snails, hermit crabs, or grazing fish to help control algae growth naturally. As your reef aquarium evolves and matures, you may wish to make changes or revisions to your aquascape to accommodate the growth of corals, fish, and other organisms. Use aquascaping tools and equipment to trim, rearrange, or add new rocks and substrate as needed, and take the opportunity to refresh the layout and design of your aquarium to keep it visually appealing and stimulating for both you and your aquatic inhabitants.

Tips and Tricks for Aquascaping Success

1. Plan Before You Start: Take the time to plan your aquascape layout and design before adding live rock and substrate to your aquarium. Sketch out different arrangements, consider the needs and preferences of your aquarium inhabitants, and visualize how the aquascape will look from various viewing angles.

2. Experiment with Texture and Contrast: Create visual interest and depth in your aquascape by incorporating a variety of textures, shapes, and colors in your live rock and substrate. Mix different types of rock formations, such as branching, encrusting, and shelf rocks, and contrast light and dark substrate materials to create dynamic and captivating landscapes.

3. Be Patient and Flexible: Aquascaping is a creative and dynamic process that requires patience, experimentation, and flexibility. Don't be afraid to try new ideas, rearrange rocks and substrate, or make adjustments to your aquascape layout as needed to achieve your desired aesthetic and functional goals. Remember that aquascaping is an ongoing journey of discovery and expression, so enjoy the process and embrace the opportunity to

create something truly unique and beautiful in your reef aquarium.

By understanding the principles of aquascaping, harnessing the benefits of live rock and substrate, and following these tips and techniques for success, you can create a stunning and functional aquascape that enhances the beauty and biodiversity of your reef aquarium. So unleash your creativity, explore different textures and layouts, and transform your underwater world into a captivating and immersive marine landscape that delights and inspires for years to come.

Adding Saltwater and R.O. Water

The quality and composition of the water in your reef aquarium are fundamental to the health and well-being of your aquatic inhabitants. Adding saltwater and R.O. (Reverse Osmosis) water to your tank is a critical step in establishing the optimal conditions for a thriving marine ecosystem. In this section, we'll explore the importance of using high-quality water, the process of mixing saltwater, the benefits of R.O. water, and tips for ensuring a successful water change regimen.

Importance of High-Quality Water

Water quality parameters such as salinity, pH, temperature, ammonia, nitrite, nitrate, alkalinity, and calcium are crucial for the health and stability of your reef aquarium. Maintaining optimal water parameters ensures the well-being of your aquarium inhabitants and supports the growth and vitality of corals, fish, and invertebrates.

The source of water used in your reef aquarium can have a significant impact on water quality and overall aquarium health. Tap water may contain impurities, chemicals, and contaminants such as chlorine, chloramine, heavy metals, and phosphates, which can harm aquatic life and promote algae growth. Using high-quality water sources such as R.O. water and

53

properly mixed saltwater helps ensure a clean and stable environment for your aquarium inhabitants.

Mixing Saltwater

Selecting the right salt mix is essential for creating high-quality saltwater for your reef aquarium. Choose a reputable brand of marine salt mix that is specifically formulated for reef aquariums and free of contaminants, additives, and fillers. Consider factors such as water parameters, coral requirements, and budget when selecting a salt mix that meets your needs.

Follow the manufacturer's instructions for mixing saltwater carefully to achieve the desired salinity and composition. Use a clean, food-grade container or mixing vessel dedicated solely to saltwater mixing, and ensure that it is free of any residues or contaminants. Add R.O. water to the container, then gradually add the appropriate amount of salt mix while stirring or circulating the water to ensure thorough dissolution. Use a reliable hydrometer or refractometer to measure the salinity of the mixed saltwater and adjust as needed to achieve the desired salinity level. The recommended salinity for a reef aquarium typically ranges from 1.024 to 1.026 specific gravity or 35 to 36 parts per thousand (ppt) on the salinity scale.

Benefits of R.O. Water

R.O. (Reverse Osmosis) water is highly purified water produced through a process of filtration and membrane technology that removes impurities, contaminants, and dissolved solids from tap water. Using R.O. water ensures a clean and consistent source of water for your reef aquarium, free of harmful substances that can affect water quality and aquatic life.

R.O. water helps reduce the risk of algae outbreaks and water quality issues by removing excess nutrients, phosphates, and organic compounds that can fuel algae growth and promote waterborne pathogens. By starting with pure R.O. water, you can minimize the need for chemical additives and treatments to maintain water quality and clarity. Marine organisms, particularly corals and invertebrates, are highly sensitive to water quality and purity. R.O. water provides a stable and suitable environment for marine life by maintaining optimal water parameters, reducing stress on aquarium inhabitants, and promoting natural growth and behavior.

Tips for Adding Saltwater and R.O. Water

1. Acclimation Process: When adding new saltwater or R.O. water to your reef aquarium, it's important to acclimate the water to match the temperature, salinity, and pH of the existing tank water. Use a drip acclimation method or slow addition technique to gradually introduce the new water over a period of time, allowing aquarium inhabitants to adjust to the change in water parameters slowly.

2. Preparation and Storage: Prepare saltwater and R.O. water in advance of water changes or top-offs to ensure consistency and reliability. Store prepared saltwater in a clean, covered container with circulation and aeration to maintain oxygen levels and prevent contamination. Keep R.O. water stored in airtight containers or reservoirs to prevent exposure to airborne pollutants and maintain purity.

3. Regular Water Testing: Monitor water parameters regularly using high-quality test kits to assess the quality and stability of your aquarium water. Test for salinity, pH, ammonia, nitrite, nitrate, alkalinity, calcium, and magnesium to ensure that water parameters remain within optimal ranges for your

aquarium inhabitants. Make adjustments as needed to maintain water quality and stability.

4. Water Change Schedule: Establish a regular water change schedule based on the needs of your reef aquarium and the recommendations of experienced hobbyists and aquarists. Perform partial water changes of 10-20% of the total volume every 1-2 weeks to replenish essential nutrients, remove accumulated waste, and maintain water quality and clarity. Adjust the frequency and volume of water changes as needed based on observed water parameters and aquarium conditions.

In Conclusion, understanding the importance of using high-quality water, mastering the process of mixing saltwater, harnessing the benefits of R.O. water, and following these tips for adding saltwater and R.O. water to your reef aquarium, you can create a clean, stable, and thriving aquatic environment for your marine inhabitants. So take the time to source and prepare high-quality water, monitor water parameters regularly, and establish a consistent water change regimen to ensure the health and vitality of your reef aquarium for years to come.

Introducing Beneficial Bacteria

Beneficial bacteria play a vital role in maintaining water quality and establishing a healthy ecosystem in your reef aquarium. Introducing these beneficial microbes is a crucial step in the setup process, as they help to establish the nitrogen cycle, break down organic waste, and promote overall water clarity and stability. In this section, we'll explore the importance of beneficial bacteria, methods for introducing them into your aquarium, and tips for optimizing their colonization and effectiveness.

Understanding Beneficial Bacteria

Beneficial bacteria are key players in the nitrogen cycle, a natural process that converts toxic ammonia and nitrite into less harmful nitrate. These bacteria colonize various surfaces within the aquarium, including live rock, substrate, and filter media, where they break down organic waste and convert ammonia into nitrite and nitrite into nitrate. Nitrate is then removed from the water through water changes, biological filtration, or chemical filtration. Beneficial bacteria provide biological filtration in the aquarium by converting harmful nitrogen compounds into less toxic forms. This process helps maintain water quality and stability by reducing ammonia and nitrite levels, which can be harmful to aquatic life at high concentrations. Establishing a healthy population of beneficial bacteria is essential for creating a stable and balanced ecosystem in your reef aquarium.

In addition to promoting water quality, beneficial bacteria play a role in supporting coral health and growth. Some species of beneficial bacteria form symbiotic relationships with corals, providing essential nutrients and promoting calcification and tissue growth. By maintaining optimal water parameters and a stable bacterial population, you can create an environment conducive to coral health and vitality.

Methods for Introducing Beneficial Bacteria

1. Seeding with Established Media: One of the most common methods for introducing beneficial bacteria into a new aquarium is to seed the tank with established filter media, live rock, or substrate from an existing, healthy aquarium. These sources contain a diverse and active population of beneficial bacteria that can help jump-start the nitrogen cycle and establish biological filtration in the new tank.

2. Commercial Bacterial Supplements: Commercial bacterial supplements are available in liquid or powdered form and contain strains of beneficial bacteria

specifically formulated for use in aquariums. These supplements can be added directly to the aquarium water or mixed with filter media or substrate to promote bacterial colonization and establishment. Follow the manufacturer's instructions for dosing and application to ensure effectiveness and safety.

3. Live Sand and Live Rock: Live sand and live rock are natural sources of beneficial bacteria that can be added to a new aquarium to introduce microbial diversity and promote bacterial colonization. Live sand contains beneficial bacteria and microorganisms that inhabit the substrate and help break down organic waste, while live rock hosts bacterial colonies that contribute to biological filtration and nutrient processing.

Tips for Optimizing Bacterial Colonization

- Provide Ample Surface Area: Beneficial bacteria require a large surface area to colonize and thrive within the aquarium. Use porous materials such as live rock, ceramic media, and bio balls in your filtration system to provide ample surface area for bacterial colonization. Maximize surface area by creating a diverse and textured aquascape with plenty of nooks, crannies, and crevices for bacteria to inhabit.

- Establish a Stable Environment: Beneficial bacteria thrive in stable and consistent water conditions, so it's essential to maintain optimal water parameters and minimize fluctuations in temperature, salinity, pH, and nutrient levels. Avoid sudden changes or disruptions to the aquarium environment that can stress or disrupt bacterial populations, and provide adequate circulation and aeration to ensure oxygenation and nutrient distribution.

- Avoid Overcleaning: While maintaining a clean and healthy aquarium is important, it's also essential to avoid overcleaning or sterilizing the tank, as this can disrupt beneficial bacterial populations. Avoid using harsh chemical cleaners or antibiotics that can kill off beneficial bacteria, and allow natural biological processes to establish and maintain water quality and clarity.

Monitoring and Maintenance

Monitor water parameters regularly using high-quality test kits to assess the effectiveness of biological filtration and ensure that beneficial bacteria are thriving in your aquarium. Test for ammonia, nitrite, nitrate, pH, alkalinity, and other relevant parameters to track the progress of the nitrogen cycle and identify any potential issues or imbalances. Some hobbyists choose to supplement beneficial bacteria populations with specialized bacterial supplements or additives designed to boost microbial growth and activity. These supplements can provide additional nutrients and substrates to support bacterial colonization and proliferation, particularly during the initial setup phase or after disruptions to the bacterial population.

Keep a close eye on your aquarium inhabitants and observe their behavior and appearance for signs of stress, illness, or water quality issues. Adjust water parameters, filtration settings, and maintenance routines as needed to address any problems or imbalances and maintain a healthy and stable environment for your reef aquarium inhabitants.

As a beginner, understanding the importance of beneficial bacteria, employing methods for introducing them into your aquarium, optimizing their colonization and effectiveness, and monitoring their progress and maintenance, you can establish a thriving and balanced ecosystem in your reef aquarium. So take the time to cultivate a healthy bacterial population, provide optimal conditions for their growth and activity, and enjoy the benefits of clean, clear, and stable water quality in your aquatic environment.

Selecting and Acclimating Livestock

Selecting and acclimating livestock is an exciting yet crucial aspect of reef aquarium keeping. Whether you're choosing fish, corals, or invertebrates, careful consideration and proper acclimation are essential for ensuring the health and compatibility of your aquarium inhabitants. In this section, we'll delve into the process of selecting and acclimating fish, corals, and invertebrates, covering important factors to consider, tips for making informed decisions, and techniques for safely introducing new additions to your reef aquarium.

Selecting Fish

Before selecting fish for your reef aquarium, research the specific requirements, behaviors, and compatibility of each species to ensure they are suitable for your tank. Consider factors such as tank size, water parameters, aggression levels, and dietary preferences when choosing fish that will coexist harmoniously with existing inhabitants.

Choose fish that are active, alert, and in good overall health at the time of purchase. Avoid specimens that show signs of illness, injury, or stress, such as lethargy, rapid breathing, abnormal swimming behavior, or visible lesions or parasites. Select fish from reputable sources with a reputation for quality and ethical

64

practices to minimize the risk of introducing diseases or parasites to your aquarium.

Consider the adult size and growth potential of fish species when selecting additions for your reef aquarium. Choose fish that will not outgrow your tank or pose a threat to smaller tankmates, corals, or invertebrates. Research the maximum size and growth rate of each species and plan accordingly to avoid overcrowding and territorial conflicts in the future. Pay attention to the behavior and temperament of fish species when selecting tankmates for your reef aquarium. Avoid pairing aggressive or territorial species with peaceful or timid fish that may become targets of aggression or harassment. Research the social dynamics and hierarchy within your chosen species to ensure compatibility and minimize stress and conflict in the aquarium.

Selecting Corals

Consider the lighting requirements and placement preferences of coral species when selecting additions for your reef aquarium. Choose corals that are compatible with your existing lighting setup and provide suitable conditions for photosynthesis and growth. Research the light intensity, spectrum, and duration required for each species to thrive and ensure proper placement within the tank.

Evaluate the water flow and circulation patterns in your reef aquarium when selecting corals, as some species prefer high-flow environments while others thrive in calmer waters. Choose corals that are adapted to the flow rates and water movement characteristics of your tank and avoid placing sensitive species in areas of excessive turbulence or dead spots.

Consider the compatibility of coral species with other inhabitants of your reef aquarium, including fish, invertebrates, and other corals. Some corals produce toxins or aggressive chemical compounds that can harm or inhibit the growth of neighboring organisms, so research the compatibility and potential interactions between corals and other tank inhabitants to avoid conflicts and promote harmony within the aquarium. Be mindful of the growth rate and expansion potential of coral species when selecting additions for your reef aquarium. Choose corals that will not outgrow their allotted space or encroach on neighboring corals, rocks, or other structures. Research the growth habits and requirements of each species and plan for adequate spacing and containment to prevent overcrowding and competition for resources.

Selecting Invertebrates

Consider the compatibility of invertebrate species with other inhabitants of your reef aquarium, including fish, corals, and other invertebrates. Some invertebrates are predatory or territorial and may pose a threat to smaller tankmates or sessile organisms, so research the behavior and compatibility of each species before introducing them to your aquarium. Choose invertebrate species that are suitable for the size and environment of your reef aquarium. Consider factors such as water parameters, substrate type, and available hiding places and shelter when selecting invertebrates that will thrive in your tank. Research the natural habitat and requirements of each species to ensure they are compatible with your aquarium setup.

Research the dietary preferences and feeding habits of invertebrate species to ensure they receive adequate nutrition in your reef aquarium. Some invertebrates are filter feeders that rely on suspended particles and plankton in the water column, while others are scavengers or detritivores that feed on organic matter and algae. Provide a varied and balanced diet to meet the nutritional needs of your invertebrates and promote health and vitality.

Acclimating Livestock

Acclimate new additions to your reef aquarium slowly to minimize stress and ensure a smooth transition to their new environment. Float the sealed bag containing the livestock in the aquarium water to equalize the temperature, then open the bag and slowly drip aquarium water into the bag over a period of 30-60 minutes using a drip acclimation line or air hose. This gradual process helps the livestock adjust to differences in water chemistry and temperature without shock or stress.

Monitor water parameters such as temperature, salinity, pH, and ammonia levels during the acclimation process to ensure they remain stable and within acceptable ranges for the livestock. Adjust water parameters as needed to match the conditions of the aquarium, taking care not to expose the livestock to sudden changes or fluctuations that can cause stress or harm.

After acclimating new livestock to your reef aquarium, observe their behavior and condition closely for signs of stress, illness, or aggression. Quarantine new additions in a separate tank or quarantine system for a period of 2-4 weeks to monitor for signs of disease or parasites and prevent the spread of pathogens to your main aquarium. This precautionary measure helps protect the health and integrity of your reef ecosystem and reduces the risk of introducing harmful organisms to established tank inhabitants.

By carefully selecting and acclimating fish, corals, and invertebrates for your reef aquarium, you can create a vibrant and harmonious underwater ecosystem that thrives for years to come. Take the time to research and choose species that are compatible with your tank environment, provide optimal conditions for their health and well-being, and acclimate them slowly and safely to their new home. With proper care and attention, your reef aquarium will become a captivating showcase of marine life and a source of joy and fascination for you and your family to enjoy.

Chapter 4

Understanding Water Parameters

Water parameters are the foundation of a healthy and thriving reef aquarium ecosystem. From temperature and salinity to pH and nutrient levels, these measurements provide valuable insights into the condition and stability of your aquarium environment. In this chapter, we will be getting in-depth knowledge on the essential water parameters that influence the health and well-being of your aquatic inhabitants, look into their significance and optimal ranges, and discuss techniques for monitoring and maintaining them effectively. By gaining a deeper understanding of water parameters, you will be better equipped to create and maintain an ideal environment for your reef aquarium inhabitants to flourish. So let's dive in and uncover the intricacies of water chemistry and its role in the success of your underwater world.

Importance of Water Quality

Water quality is paramount in maintaining a thriving and sustainable reef aquarium ecosystem. The quality of the water directly impacts the health and well-being of your aquatic inhabitants, influencing everything from growth and reproduction to disease resistance and behavior. In this section, we'll get to know the importance of water quality in a reef aquarium, discussing its role in supporting life, promoting coral growth, and maintaining overall ecosystem balance.

Supporting Life

High water quality is essential for creating an environment that supports the diverse array of life found in a reef aquarium, including fish, corals, invertebrates, and microorganisms. Maintaining stable water parameters such as temperature, salinity, pH, and nutrient levels ensures the health and vitality of aquarium inhabitants, allowing them to thrive and exhibit natural behaviors.

Poor water quality can stress aquarium inhabitants and weaken their immune systems, making them more susceptible to diseases, infections, and parasites. By providing clean, well-oxygenated water with balanced parameters, you can minimize stress on fish and other organisms, reduce the risk of illness, and promote overall health and resilience in your reef aquarium community.

Optimal water quality conditions are conducive to reproduction and growth in aquarium organisms, allowing them to breed successfully and develop into healthy adults. Stable water parameters and pristine water quality provide a favorable environment for spawning, larval development, and juvenile growth, supporting population sustainability and genetic diversity within the aquarium.

Supporting Coral Growth

Coral health and growth are closely tied to water chemistry parameters such as calcium, alkalinity, and magnesium levels. These elements are essential for skeletal formation, coral tissue growth, and the deposition of calcium carbonate skeletons, which are the building blocks of coral reefs. Maintaining stable and balanced levels of calcium, alkalinity, and magnesium is critical for promoting coral growth and calcification in the reef aquarium.

Water quality also plays a role in supporting coral photosynthesis, the process by which corals and symbiotic algae (zooxanthellae) produce energy using sunlight. Clean, clear water with optimal light penetration promotes photosynthetic activity in corals, providing them with the energy they need to grow, reproduce, and maintain vibrant colors. Poor water quality, excessive algae growth, or sedimentation can hinder light penetration and inhibit coral photosynthesis, leading to decreased growth and vitality in reef aquarium corals.

Controlling nutrient levels such as nitrate and phosphate is crucial for preventing nutrient imbalances and promoting healthy coral growth in the reef aquarium. Excessive nutrient levels can fuel algae growth, which competes with corals for light and space and can smother coral colonies. By maintaining low nutrient levels through proper filtration, nutrient export, and water changes, you can create a nutrient-limited environment that encourages coral growth and maintains water clarity in your reef aquarium.

Maintaining Ecosystem Balance

Water quality management is closely linked to the nitrogen cycle, a biological process that converts toxic ammonia and nitrite into less harmful nitrate. Beneficial bacteria play a crucial role in the nitrogen cycle by colonizing various surfaces within the aquarium and breaking down organic waste. By establishing and maintaining a healthy population of beneficial bacteria, you can ensure effective biological filtration and maintain water quality and stability in your reef aquarium.

Adequate oxygenation and gas exchange are essential for maintaining water quality and supporting aerobic respiration in aquarium organisms. Proper water movement, surface agitation, and aeration help oxygenate the water column and remove excess carbon dioxide, ensuring that fish, corals, and other organisms receive an adequate supply of oxygen for respiration. By promoting efficient gas exchange, you can prevent oxygen depletion, reduce the risk of respiratory stress, and maintain optimal water quality in your reef aquarium.

pH stability is critical for maintaining water quality and supporting biological processes in the reef aquarium. Fluctuations in pH can stress aquarium inhabitants and disrupt biological functions such as nutrient uptake, enzyme activity, and calcification in corals. By buffering water chemistry and stabilizing pH within the optimal range for reef organisms, you can create a stable and supportive environment that promotes health, growth, and vitality throughout the aquarium ecosystem.

In conclusion, water quality is of paramount importance in a reef aquarium, influencing the health, growth, and sustainability of aquarium inhabitants and coral reef ecosystems. By understanding the significance of water quality parameters, monitoring and maintaining water quality diligently, and implementing effective strategies for nutrient management and biological filtration, you can create a pristine and thriving aquatic environment that delights the senses and fosters the growth and well-being of your reef aquarium community.

Monitoring Water Parameters

Regular monitoring of water parameters is essential for maintaining a healthy and stable reef aquarium environment. By assessing key parameters such as temperature, salinity, pH, ammonia, nitrite, nitrate, alkalinity, calcium, and magnesium, aquarists can ensure optimal conditions for their aquatic inhabitants and prevent potential problems before they arise. In this section, we'll gain knowledge on each of these water parameters in detail, discussing their significance, optimal ranges, monitoring techniques, and strategies for maintaining stability.

Temperature

Temperature plays a crucial role in the health and well-being of reef aquarium inhabitants, influencing metabolic rates, immune function, and behavior. Sudden fluctuations or extremes in temperature can stress aquarium organisms and compromise their health and vitality. The optimal temperature range for most reef aquariums is typically between 75°F and 82°F (24°C to 28°C). It's essential to maintain stable temperatures within this range to ensure the comfort and stability of aquarium inhabitants.

Use a reliable aquarium thermometer to monitor water temperature regularly and ensure it remains within the optimal range for your reef aquarium. Place the thermometer in a central location within the tank away from direct sunlight, heaters, or other heat sources to obtain an accurate reading of the water temperature. Maintain stable temperatures by using quality aquarium heaters and controllers to regulate temperature fluctuations and prevent overheating or chilling. Monitor ambient room temperature and adjust aquarium heating or cooling equipment as needed to maintain optimal conditions for your aquarium inhabitants.

Salinity

Salinity, or the concentration of dissolved salts in the water, is critical for maintaining osmotic balance and physiological function in marine organisms. Fluctuations in salinity can stress aquarium inhabitants and disrupt their internal water balance. The optimal salinity range for most reef aquariums is typically between 1.024 and 1.026 specific gravity or 35 to 36 parts per thousand (ppt) on the salinity scale. It's essential to maintain stable salinity levels within this range to support the health and vitality of marine organisms. Use a reliable hydrometer, refractometer, or conductivity meter to measure salinity accurately and monitor changes in water salinity over time. Calibrate your salinity measurement device regularly to ensure accurate readings and adjust for temperature variations if necessary.

Maintain stable salinity levels by regularly topping off evaporated water with freshwater or saltwater to compensate for water loss. Perform regular water changes using pre-mixed saltwater to replenish essential elements and maintain stable salinity levels in the aquarium.

pH

pH measures the acidity or alkalinity of the water and plays a crucial role in biological processes such as nutrient uptake, enzyme activity, and calcification in corals. Fluctuations in pH can stress aquarium inhabitants and inhibit their ability to thrive and reproduce. The optimal pH range for most reef aquariums is typically between 8.1 and 8.4. It's essential to maintain stable pH levels within this range to support the health and growth of marine organisms and promote a stable and balanced aquarium ecosystem. Use a reliable pH test kit or pH monitor to measure water pH regularly and monitor changes in pH over time. Test pH at the same time each day and in multiple locations within the aquarium to obtain accurate and representative readings. Maintain stable pH levels by buffering water chemistry and stabilizing pH fluctuations using commercial buffer products or natural buffering agents such as aragonite sand or crushed coral substrate. Avoid sudden changes in pH by performing gradual adjustments and monitoring water parameters closely during maintenance activities.

Ammonia, Nitrite, and Nitrate

Ammonia, nitrite, and nitrate are nitrogenous compounds that are produced as byproducts of organic waste decomposition and biological processes in the aquarium. Elevated levels of ammonia and nitrite can be toxic to aquarium inhabitants, while high nitrate levels can fuel algae growth and inhibit coral health and growth. Ammonia and nitrite levels should be undetectable (0 ppm) in a well-established reef aquarium, while nitrate levels should be kept below 10-20 ppm to prevent algae outbreaks and maintain water quality. Use reliable test kits or electronic monitors to measure ammonia, nitrite, and nitrate levels regularly and monitor changes in nitrogenous compound concentrations over time. Test water parameters before and after water changes, feeding, and maintenance activities to assess their impact on water quality. Maintain low ammonia, nitrite, and nitrate levels by performing regular water changes, optimizing filtration, and minimizing organic waste accumulation in the aquarium. Use protein skimmers, biological filtration, and chemical filtration media to remove excess nutrients and maintain water quality and clarity.

Alkalinity

Alkalinity, or carbonate hardness (KH), measures the concentration of carbonate and bicarbonate ions in the water and influences pH stability, coral growth, and calcification. Fluctuations in alkalinity can affect coral health and lead to pH swings in the aquarium. The optimal alkalinity range for most reef aquariums is typically between 7 and 11 dKH (degrees of carbonate hardness). It's essential to maintain stable alkalinity levels within this range to support coral growth and maintain pH stability in the aquarium. Use a reliable alkalinity test kit or electronic monitor to measure alkalinity levels regularly and monitor changes in carbonate hardness over time. Test alkalinity weekly or bi-weekly and adjust alkalinity as needed to maintain stable levels in the aquarium. Maintain stable alkalinity levels by replenishing alkalinity through regular water changes, supplementation with alkalinity buffers or additives, and monitoring alkalinity consumption by corals and other organisms. Monitor pH closely when adjusting alkalinity to prevent pH swings and maintain water chemistry stability.

Calcium and Magnesium

Calcium and magnesium are essential elements for coral growth, skeletal formation, and overall health in the reef aquarium. These elements play a critical role in supporting coral calcification, tissue growth, and coloration. The optimal calcium level for most reef aquariums is typically between 400 and 450 ppm (parts per million), while magnesium levels should be maintained between 1250 and 1350 ppm. It's essential to maintain stable calcium and magnesium levels within these ranges to support coral growth and maintain water chemistry balance. Use reliable test kits or electronic monitors to measure calcium and magnesium levels regularly and monitor changes in elemental concentrations over time. Test calcium and magnesium levels weekly or bi-weekly and adjust supplementation as needed to maintain stable levels in the aquarium. Maintain stable calcium and magnesium levels by supplementing with commercial calcium and magnesium additives, performing regular water changes with pre-mixed saltwater, and monitoring coral growth and coloration as indicators of elemental balance. Monitor alkalinity levels closely when adjusting calcium and magnesium to maintain proper stoichiometric balance and prevent precipitation or depletion of calcium carbonate.

By monitoring these key water parameters regularly and maintaining stable conditions within optimal ranges, aquarists can create a healthy and thriving reef aquarium environment that supports the growth and well-being of their aquatic inhabitants. So take the time to monitor water parameters diligently, make adjustments as needed, and provide your reef aquarium community with the optimal conditions they need to flourish and thrive.

Adjusting Water Parameters

Maintaining optimal water parameters is crucial for the health and stability of a reef aquarium ecosystem. However, achieving and maintaining these parameters within the ideal ranges can sometimes require adjustments. In this section, we'll look at the various methods and techniques for adjusting water parameters such as temperature, salinity, pH, ammonia, nitrite, nitrate, alkalinity, calcium, and magnesium. By understanding these adjustment methods, aquarists can effectively manage and optimize their reef aquarium environment to promote the health and well-being of their aquatic inhabitants.

Adjusting Temperature

The primary method for adjusting aquarium temperature is by using heating or cooling equipment, such as aquarium heaters or chillers. Aquarium heaters maintain water temperature by heating the water to the desired setpoint, while chillers cool the water when temperatures rise above the desired range. Use a reliable temperature controller to regulate heating or cooling equipment and maintain stable water temperatures within the optimal range for your reef aquarium. Set the temperature controller to the desired temperature range and monitor temperature fluctuations to ensure consistent and reliable performance.

Position aquarium heaters and chillers strategically within the aquarium to distribute heat or cold evenly throughout the water column. Insulate external equipment such as heaters and plumbing to minimize heat loss and improve energy efficiency, especially in larger or open-top aquariums where heat dissipation may be more significant.

Adjusting Salinity

Regular water changes with pre-mixed saltwater are the most effective method for adjusting salinity in a reef aquarium. Perform partial water changes using saltwater with the desired salinity level to replenish essential elements and maintain stable salinity levels within the optimal range. Use an automatic top-off (ATO) system to replenish evaporated water with freshwater or saltwater as needed to maintain stable salinity levels in the aquarium. ATO systems can help prevent fluctuations in salinity caused by evaporation and ensure consistency in water chemistry. Use a reliable hydrometer, refractometer, or conductivity meter to measure salinity accurately and monitor changes in water salinity over time. Adjust salinity by adding freshwater or saltwater to the aquarium as needed to achieve the desired specific gravity or salinity level.

Adjusting pH

Use commercial alkalinity buffers or pH-adjusting products to stabilize pH and maintain alkalinity levels within the optimal range for your reef aquarium. Buffering agents contain bicarbonate and carbonate ions that help neutralize acids and stabilize pH in the aquarium. Utilize a calcium reactor to supplement alkalinity and maintain stable pH levels in the reef aquarium. Calcium reactors dissolve calcium carbonate media to release calcium and carbonate ions into the water, which helps buffer pH and replenish alkalinity over time.

Increase aeration and surface agitation in the aquarium to improve gas exchange and oxygenation and stabilize pH levels. Air stones, powerheads, and surface skimmers can help increase water movement and promote gas exchange, which can help stabilize pH and prevent fluctuations.

Adjusting Ammonia, Nitrite, and Nitrate

Enhance biological filtration in the aquarium by optimizing filtration media, increasing surface area for beneficial bacteria colonization, and promoting the growth of nitrifying bacteria. Biological filtration converts toxic ammonia and nitrite into less harmful nitrate, reducing nitrogenous compound levels in the aquarium. Use a protein skimmer to remove organic waste, dissolved organic compounds, and excess nutrients from the water column, including ammonia, nitrite, and dissolved organic nitrogen. Protein skimming can help reduce nutrient levels and improve water quality in the reef aquarium.

Perform regular water changes with high-quality saltwater to dilute nitrate levels and remove accumulated organic waste from the aquarium. Water changes replenish essential elements, export excess nutrients, and maintain stable water chemistry and nutrient levels in the aquarium.

Adjusting Alkalinity, Calcium, and Magnesium

Use commercial alkalinity, calcium, and magnesium supplements to replenish depleted elements and maintain stable levels in the reef aquarium. Follow manufacturer guidelines for dosing and adjust supplementation based on water testing results and coral growth and coloration.

Employ a calcium reactor to supplement alkalinity, calcium, and magnesium in the aquarium by dissolving calcium carbonate media and releasing essential elements into the water. Calcium reactors provide a continuous source of calcium, alkalinity, and magnesium, promoting coral growth and calcification in the reef aquarium.

Perform regular water changes with pre-mixed saltwater to replenish alkalinity, calcium, and magnesium levels and maintain stable elemental ratios in the aquarium. Water changes help remove accumulated pollutants and replenish essential elements, supporting coral health and growth in the reef aquarium.

By employing these methods and techniques for adjusting water parameters in your reef aquarium, you can effectively manage and optimize the aquatic environment to support the health, growth, and vitality of your aquatic inhabitants. Regular monitoring, careful observation, and proactive adjustments will help you maintain stable water chemistry and create a thriving reef aquarium ecosystem for years to come.

Chapter 5

Feeding and Nutrition

Feeding and nutrition play a vital role in the health and well-being of the inhabitants of a reef aquarium. Proper nutrition is essential for supporting growth, immune function, coloration, and reproduction in fish, corals, and invertebrates. In this chapter, we will gain insights on the importance of feeding and nutrition in a reef aquarium, discuss the dietary requirements of different organisms, and provide guidance on selecting and offering appropriate foods. Whether you're caring for fish, corals, or invertebrates, understanding their nutritional needs and implementing a balanced feeding regimen is essential for maintaining a vibrant and thriving reef aquarium ecosystem. So let's dive into the fascinating world of feeding and nutrition and uncover the secrets to nourishing your underwater community for optimal health and vitality.

Feeding Fish

Feeding fish in a reef aquarium is not only about providing sustenance but also about promoting health, vitality, and natural behaviors. In this section, we'll see the various aspects of feeding fish in a reef aquarium, including dietary requirements, feeding strategies, and tips for ensuring a balanced and nutritious diet for your finned friends.

Understanding Fish Dietary Requirements

Fish in a reef aquarium can have diverse dietary preferences, ranging from omnivorous to herbivorous and carnivorous. Understanding the natural feeding habits of your fish species is essential for selecting appropriate foods and meeting their nutritional needs.

Fish require a balanced diet that provides essential nutrients such as proteins, carbohydrates, lipids (fats), vitamins, and minerals. Protein-rich foods support growth and muscle development, carbohydrates provide energy, and lipids supply essential fatty acids for metabolic functions. Offering a variety of foods ensures that fish receive a balanced and nutritious diet that meets their dietary requirements. Include a mix of live, frozen, and dry foods such as pellets, flakes, and granules to provide a diverse range of nutrients and stimulate natural feeding behaviors.

Feeding Strategies for Reef Aquarium Fish

Feed fish small, frequent meals throughout the day to mimic their natural feeding patterns and prevent overfeeding. Monitor fish behavior and appetite to determine the appropriate feeding frequency and adjust portion sizes accordingly to prevent wastage and maintain water quality.

Use target feeding techniques to ensure that all fish receive their share of food and prevent aggressive feeders from monopolizing the feeding process. Use feeding rings, feeding stations, or feeding tongs to deliver food directly to individual fish or specific areas of the aquarium. Choose foods that are suitable for the feeding habits and preferences of your fish species. Slow-sinking pellets or flakes are ideal for mid-water and bottom-dwelling species, while floating foods are suitable for surface-feeders and species that prefer to feed from the water's surface.

Selecting and Offering Fish Foods

Commercial Fish Foods: Choose high-quality commercial fish foods that are specifically formulated for marine fish species. Look for foods that contain a balanced mix of proteins, vitamins, and minerals and avoid products with excessive fillers, artificial colors, and preservatives. Supplement commercial fish foods with live and frozen foods to provide additional nutrition and enrichment for your fish. Offer live foods such as brine shrimp, mysis shrimp, and copepods as occasional treats to stimulate natural hunting behaviors and provide essential nutrients.

Consider preparing homemade fish foods using fresh and nutritious ingredients to provide a custom-tailored diet for your fish. Recipes can include a combination of seafood, vegetables, and supplements blended into a nutritious fish paste or gel that can be portioned and frozen for future use.

Observing and Monitoring Fish Feeding Behavior

Observe fish feeding behavior closely to assess appetite, activity level, and feeding preferences. Healthy fish will exhibit active feeding behavior, eagerly consuming food offered to them, while stressed or sick fish may show reduced appetite or lethargy.

Monitor the aquarium for uneaten food and waste accumulation to prevent water quality issues. Remove uneaten food promptly to prevent fouling of the water and adjust feeding quantities as needed to minimize waste and maintain water quality. Regular feeding is essential for maintaining fish health and condition, promoting growth, and enhancing coloration. Monitor fish body condition, fin health, and coloration to assess overall health and adjust feeding practices as needed to support optimal health and vitality.

As an aquarist, understanding the dietary requirements of your fish species, implementing appropriate feeding strategies, and offering a balanced and nutritious diet, you can ensure the health, vitality, and well-being of your reef aquarium fish. Take the time to observe and monitor fish feeding behavior, select high-quality foods, and provide variety and enrichment to promote natural behaviors and support a thriving aquatic community.

Feeding Corals and Invertebrates

Feeding corals and invertebrates in a reef aquarium is essential for promoting growth, coloration, and overall health. While many corals and invertebrates rely primarily on photosynthesis for energy, supplemental feeding can provide additional nutrients and support optimal nutrition. This section showcases the fascinating world of feeding corals and invertebrates, exploring their dietary requirements, feeding strategies, and techniques for enhancing their health and vitality.

Understanding Coral and Invertebrate Dietary Requirements

Corals and many invertebrates have developed symbiotic relationships with photosynthetic algae called zooxanthellae, which provide them with energy through photosynthesis. However, corals also require additional nutrients such as amino acids, fatty acids, and micronutrients to support growth and tissue repair. Some corals and invertebrates are filter feeders, capturing planktonic organisms and organic particles from the water column to supplement their nutritional needs. These organisms use specialized structures such as tentacles, polyps, or mucus nets to capture prey and extract nutrients.

Certain corals and invertebrates are capable of directly consuming food particles, such as zooplankton, phytoplankton, and small prey items. Direct feeding allows these organisms to obtain essential nutrients and energy directly from prey capture, supplementing their energy requirements and supporting growth and reproduction.

Feeding Strategies for Corals and Invertebrates

Broadcast feeding involves adding liquid or powdered coral foods to the aquarium water to provide nutrition for filter-feeding corals and invertebrates. These foods contain a blend of planktonic organisms, amino acids, vitamins, and other nutrients to support coral health and growth.

Target feeding involves delivering food directly to individual corals and invertebrates to ensure that they receive their share of nutrition. Use specialized feeding tools such as pipettes, turkey basters, or feeding syringes to deliver food to specific organisms without overfeeding the entire aquarium.

Create feeding stations or areas within the aquarium where corals and invertebrates can gather to consume food more efficiently. Place feeding dishes, trays, or platforms near coral colonies or invertebrate habitats and offer food directly to these designated feeding areas.

Selecting and Offering Foods for Corals and Invertebrates

Choose high-quality liquid coral foods that contain a blend of planktonic organisms, amino acids, vitamins, and minerals to support coral health and growth. Look for products that are specifically formulated for reef aquarium corals and invertebrates and contain natural ingredients without artificial additives. Consider using powdered coral foods that can be mixed with aquarium water to create a suspension of nutritious particles for filter-feeding corals and invertebrates. These foods can be broadcast into the water column or target fed to specific organisms using feeding tools.

Supplement commercial coral foods with frozen planktonic organisms such as copepods, brine shrimp, and rotifers to provide additional nutrition and enrichment for corals and invertebrates. Thaw frozen foods in aquarium water before adding them to the aquarium to ensure optimal nutrient delivery.

Observing and Monitoring Feeding Responses

Observe coral and invertebrate feeding responses closely to assess appetite, activity level, and feeding preferences. Healthy corals and invertebrates will extend feeding tentacles, polyps, or mucus nets to capture prey and actively consume food particles.

Regular feeding can enhance coral growth, tissue expansion, and coloration, providing visible indicators of improved health and vitality. Monitor coral polyp extension, tissue expansion, and color intensity to assess the effectiveness of feeding practices and adjust feeding frequency and types of food offered as needed. Establish a feeding schedule based on the nutritional requirements and feeding behaviors of corals and invertebrates in your reef aquarium. Feed corals and invertebrates small, frequent meals throughout the week to ensure consistent nutrient availability and promote optimal health and growth.

By understanding the dietary requirements of corals and invertebrates, implementing appropriate feeding strategies, and offering a balanced and nutritious diet, you can support the health, growth, and vitality of these fascinating organisms in your reef aquarium. Take the time to observe and monitor feeding responses, select high-quality foods, and provide variety and enrichment to promote natural behaviors and enhance the beauty of your aquatic ecosystem.

Supplementing with Phytoplankton and Zooplankton

Supplementing reef aquariums with phytoplankton and zooplankton is a popular practice among hobbyists aiming to enhance nutrition and support the health of corals, invertebrates, and filter-feeding organisms. In this section, you'll get to know, the benefits of supplementing with phytoplankton and zooplankton, discuss the types of organisms involved, and provide guidance on incorporating these supplements into your reef aquarium regimen.

Benefits of Phytoplankton and Zooplankton Supplements

Phytoplankton and zooplankton are rich sources of essential nutrients, including vitamins, minerals, proteins, and fatty acids, which can supplement the diet of corals, invertebrates, and filter-feeding organisms in the reef aquarium. These supplements provide a natural and nutritious food source that supports growth, coloration, and overall health. Phytoplankton supplements can support photosynthetic organisms such as corals and clams by providing additional energy and nutrients for photosynthesis. Phytoplankton contains chlorophyll and other pigments that capture light energy, supporting the production of carbohydrates and oxygen through photosynthesis.

Zooplankton supplements serve as prey for filter-feeding organisms such as corals, clams, sponges, and feather dusters, which capture planktonic organisms from the water column to supplement their nutritional needs. Zooplankton provides a natural and diverse food source that stimulates natural feeding behaviors and promotes health and vitality.

Types of Phytoplankton and Zooplankton Supplements

- Phytoplankton: Phytoplankton supplements typically consist of single-celled algae such as Nannochloropsis, Tetraselmis, and Isochrysis, which are cultured and harvested for use in reef aquariums. These microalgae are rich in proteins, carbohydrates, vitamins, and pigments that support the nutritional needs of corals, clams, and other filter-feeding organisms.

- Zooplankton: Zooplankton supplements include small, planktonic organisms such as copepods, rotifers, and amphipods, which serve as prey for filter-feeding organisms in the reef aquarium. Live zooplankton cultures or frozen zooplankton products are available commercially and can be used to supplement the diet of corals, clams, and other invertebrates.

Incorporating Phytoplankton and Zooplankton into the Aquarium Regimen

Incorporate phytoplankton and zooplankton supplements into your reef aquarium feeding regimen by adding them to the aquarium periodically throughout the week. Offer phytoplankton supplements during the day to support photosynthetic organisms, while zooplankton supplements can be added in the evening to coincide with nocturnal feeding behaviors. Phytoplankton supplements can be added directly to the aquarium water or target fed to corals and invertebrates using a pipette, syringe, or dosing pump. Zooplankton supplements can be broadcast into the water column or target fed to specific organisms using a feeding tool or baster to ensure efficient delivery and consumption.

Monitor the response of corals, invertebrates, and other aquarium inhabitants to phytoplankton and zooplankton supplements to assess their effectiveness and adjust feeding practices as needed. Observe feeding behavior, polyp extension, tissue expansion, and coloration to evaluate the impact of supplements on overall health and vitality.

Culturing Phytoplankton and Zooplankton at Home

- Phytoplankton Culture: Culturing phytoplankton at home allows hobbyists to produce a continuous supply of fresh phytoplankton for supplementation. Set up a phytoplankton culture using a suitable vessel, such as a glass jar or culture flask, and provide light, nutrients, and aeration to promote algae growth.

- Zooplankton Culture: Culturing zooplankton at home enables hobbyists to maintain live zooplankton cultures for feeding corals, invertebrates, and small fish. Start a zooplankton culture using a culture vessel with suitable filtration and provide live phytoplankton or commercial zooplankton feed to support zooplankton growth and reproduction.

Feed phytoplankton and zooplankton cultures regularly with appropriate nutrients and monitor growth and population density over time. Harvest mature phytoplankton cultures by siphoning or decanting dense algal cultures, and harvest zooplankton cultures using a fine mesh sieve or net to collect live organisms for feeding to aquarium inhabitants. Incorporating phytoplankton and zooplankton supplements into your reef aquarium regimen can provide valuable nutritional enrichment and support the health and vitality of corals, invertebrates, and filter-feeding organisms. Experiment with different types of supplements, feeding techniques, and feeding schedules to find the optimal combination that meets the dietary needs of your aquarium inhabitants and promotes a thriving reef ecosystem.

Chapter 6

Maintenance and Care

Maintaining a healthy and thriving reef aquarium requires dedication, attention to detail, and a proactive approach to aquarium maintenance. In this chapter, we will get to know, the essential aspects of maintaining and caring for your reef aquarium, covering everything from water quality management to equipment maintenance and coral husbandry. By establishing a comprehensive maintenance routine and implementing best practices for aquarium care, you can create an optimal environment for your aquatic inhabitants to flourish and thrive. So let's explore the key principles of maintenance and care that will help you maintain a beautiful and sustainable reef aquarium ecosystem for years to come.

Regular Water Changes

Regular water changes are a fundamental aspect of maintaining a healthy and balanced reef aquarium environment. In this section, we'll explore the importance of water changes, discuss the benefits they provide, and provide guidance on how to perform them effectively to promote the well-being of your aquatic inhabitants.

Importance of Water Changes

Over time, organic waste, uneaten food, and metabolic byproducts can accumulate in the aquarium water, leading to deteriorating water quality. Regular water changes help dilute these pollutants, reducing their concentration and minimizing the risk of water quality issues such as ammonia spikes, nitrite spikes, and high nitrate levels.

Water changes remove dissolved organic compounds, excess nutrients, and accumulated debris from the aquarium water, promoting a cleaner and healthier aquatic environment. By exporting nutrients that can fuel algae growth and inhibit coral health, water changes help maintain optimal water quality and support coral growth and vitality. In addition to removing pollutants and excess nutrients, water changes replenish essential elements and trace elements that may become depleted over time.

104

Freshwater used for water changes typically contains essential minerals and ions that support coral growth, calcification, and coloration, ensuring a stable and balanced aquarium environment.

Benefits of Regular Water Changes

- Improved Water Clarity: Water changes help improve water clarity by removing suspended particles, dissolved organics, and other debris that can cloud the water and reduce visibility. Clear water not only enhances the visual appeal of the aquarium but also allows light to penetrate deeper, supporting photosynthesis and coral health.

- Stabilized Water Parameters: By maintaining stable water parameters through regular water changes, aquarists can create a more resilient and balanced aquarium environment that is less prone to fluctuations and stressors. Stable water parameters support the health and well-being of aquarium inhabitants, promoting natural behaviors, growth, and reproduction.

- Reduced Algae Growth: Water changes help control algae growth by removing excess nutrients and organic matter that can fuel algal blooms. By maintaining low nutrient levels and optimal water quality, water changes create an environment that is less favorable for algae growth, allowing corals and other desirable organisms to thrive.

Performing Effective Water Changes

Determine the appropriate frequency and volume of water changes based on the size of your aquarium, stocking levels, and nutrient levels. As a general guideline, aim to perform water changes of 10-20% of the total aquarium volume every 1-2 weeks to maintain optimal water quality and support coral health. Before performing a water change, prepare fresh saltwater using a high-quality marine salt mix and a reliable source of RO/DI (reverse osmosis/deionized) water. Mix the saltwater thoroughly to ensure complete dissolution and achieve a consistent salinity level that matches the aquarium's existing water parameters.

Use a siphon or aquarium vacuum to remove debris, detritus, and uneaten food from the substrate during water changes. As you siphon out old water, simultaneously refill the aquarium with freshly prepared saltwater to maintain water level and minimize stress on aquarium inhabitants. Match the temperature and salinity of the newly prepared saltwater to that of the aquarium water to avoid temperature shock and stress on the inhabitants.

Allow the fresh saltwater to acclimate to the aquarium temperature before adding it to the tank to prevent sudden fluctuations in water parameters.

After performing a water change, monitor water parameters such as temperature, salinity, pH, ammonia, nitrite, and nitrate to ensure stability and assess the impact of the water change on water quality. Regular testing allows you to detect and address any issues promptly, ensuring the continued health and well-being of your aquarium inhabitants.

Cleaning and Maintenance Tasks

Regular cleaning and maintenance are essential for preserving water quality, promoting the health of aquatic inhabitants, and enhancing the overall aesthetics of a reef aquarium. In this section, we'll look at a variety of cleaning and maintenance tasks that are necessary for keeping your aquarium in optimal condition. From algae removal to equipment maintenance, we'll cover everything you need to know to ensure the long-term success of your reef ecosystem.

Algae Management

Algae growth is a common occurrence in reef aquariums and can manifest in various forms, including green algae, diatoms, cyanobacteria (red slime algae), and nuisance algae such as hair algae and bubble algae. Understanding the different types of algae and their causes is essential for effective management and control. Use a scraper, brush, or algae magnet to manually remove algae from aquarium glass, rocks, and other surfaces. Regular maintenance of algae-prone areas helps prevent excessive growth and maintains the visual clarity of the aquarium.

Introduce herbivorous fish, snails, and invertebrates that graze on algae as part of your cleanup crew.

108

Species such as tangs, blennies, and certain snail species can help keep algae growth in check by consuming algae and grazing on surfaces. In cases of persistent algae outbreaks, consider using chemical treatments such as algae-control additives or aquarium-safe algaecides. However, exercise caution when using chemicals, as they can affect water quality and harm sensitive organisms if used improperly.

Substrate Maintenance

Use a gravel vacuum or siphon to remove debris, detritus, and uneaten food from the substrate during water changes. Regular vacuuming prevents the buildup of organic waste, which can contribute to nutrient imbalances and poor water quality. Periodically stir the substrate to prevent anaerobic pockets from forming, which can lead to the production of toxic gases such as hydrogen sulfide. Aeration of the substrate helps promote beneficial aerobic bacteria activity and prevents the accumulation of organic matter.

Inspect the substrate for areas of excessive detritus accumulation or dead spots and perform targeted cleaning as needed. Use a turkey baster or gentle water flow to dislodge debris and detritus from hard-to-reach areas without disturbing the substrate bed.

Equipment Maintenance

Regularly clean and maintain filtration equipment such as mechanical filters, protein skimmers, and filter media to ensure optimal performance. Rinse mechanical filters and replace filter media according to manufacturer recommendations to prevent clogging and maintain water flow. Clean and inspect aquarium pumps, powerheads, and circulation pumps regularly to remove debris and prevent impeller blockages. Lubricate pump components as needed and replace worn or damaged parts to maintain efficiency and reliability.

Clean aquarium lighting fixtures, reflectors, and lenses to remove dust, algae, and mineral deposits that can reduce light penetration and intensity. Replace outdated bulbs or LED modules to maintain proper spectrum and intensity for coral growth and coloration. Check aquarium heaters periodically to ensure proper functioning and accuracy of temperature settings. Clean heater surfaces and adjust thermostat settings as needed to maintain stable water temperature within the desired range.

Coral Husbandry

Trim overgrown corals and perform coral fragging (fragmentation) to manage coral growth and propagation. Use specialized coral-cutting tools and fragging kits to safely divide coral colonies into smaller fragments for propagation or to control size and shape. Supplement coral nutrition with targeted feeding of coral foods, amino acids, and trace elements to support growth, coloration, and polyp extension. Broadcast liquid coral foods or target-feed coral polyps with specialized feeding tools to ensure efficient nutrient delivery.

Adjust water flow patterns and placement of powerheads and wavemakers to provide adequate water movement and circulation around coral colonies. Optimizing water flow helps remove debris, facilitates nutrient uptake, and prevents sediment buildup on coral surfaces. Regularly inspect corals for signs of stress, disease, or predation and take appropriate action to address any issues promptly. Monitor coral coloration, polyp extension, tissue recession, and growth rates to assess overall health and vitality.

By incorporating these cleaning and maintenance tasks into your reef aquarium care routine, you can create a clean, healthy, and visually appealing aquatic environment for your coral, fish, and invertebrate inhabitants. Regular upkeep not only preserves water quality and promotes organism health but also enhances the enjoyment and satisfaction of maintaining a thriving reef ecosystem.

Troubleshooting Common Issues

In the dynamic world of reef aquariums, aquarists may encounter various challenges ranging from algae outbreaks to coral diseases and pest infestations. In this section, we'll address common issues faced by reef aquarium hobbyists and provide practical guidance on troubleshooting and resolving these challenges effectively.

Algae Control

Before implementing control measures, it's crucial to identify the type of algae present in the aquarium. Different algae species may require different management strategies, so understanding the specific characteristics of the algae is essential.

Algae growth is often fueled by excess nutrients such as nitrates and phosphates. Implement strategies to reduce nutrient levels, such as increasing water changes, improving filtration, and limiting feeding quantities. Additionally, consider adding nutrient-consuming organisms like macroalgae or enhancing biological filtration to help control nutrient levels.

Adjusting lighting intensity and duration can help control algae growth, especially for photosynthetic algae species. Reduce the photoperiod or intensity of light if excessive algae growth is observed, and ensure that lighting spectrums are appropriate for coral health while discouraging algae proliferation.

Introducing algae-eating organisms such as herbivorous fish, snails, and hermit crabs can help naturally control algae growth. Choose species known for their grazing behavior and compatibility with your existing aquarium inhabitants to avoid overstocking or aggression issues.

Disease Management

Implement a quarantine protocol for new additions to the aquarium to prevent the introduction of pathogens and parasites. Quarantine newly acquired fish and invertebrates in a separate tank for observation and treatment before introducing them to the main display aquarium. Regularly observe aquarium inhabitants for signs of disease, including abnormal behavior, changes in appetite, visible lesions, or unusual growths. Early detection allows for prompt intervention and treatment, minimizing the spread of disease and reducing its impact on the aquarium ecosystem.

Depending on the type and severity of the disease, various treatment options may be available, including medications, freshwater dips, and dietary supplements. Research the specific requirements and potential side effects of each treatment method before implementation, and follow dosing instructions carefully to avoid harming sensitive organisms.

Maintaining stable water parameters and minimizing stressors can help prevent disease outbreaks and support the immune health of aquarium inhabitants. Ensure adequate water flow, filtration, and oxygenation, and avoid overcrowding or aggressive interactions among tankmates.

Dealing with Coral Pests

Familiarize yourself with common coral pests such as flatworms, nudibranchs, bristle worms, and Aiptasia anemones. Regularly inspect corals for signs of pest infestations, including tissue damage, unusual growths, or presence of pests on coral surfaces. For visible pests such as Aiptasia anemones or bristle worms, manual removal may be an effective control method. Use specialized tools or traps to safely remove pests from coral colonies without causing harm to the corals themselves.

Introduce natural predators or competitors of coral pests to help control their populations. For example, peppermint shrimp are known to feed on Aiptasia anemones, while certain wrasses and filefish may consume flatworms and nudibranchs.

Chemical treatments such as Aiptasia-specific solutions or pest control dips can be used to target stubborn pest infestations. However, exercise caution when using chemicals, as they can have unintended consequences and may harm sensitive corals or other aquarium inhabitants if not used properly.

By addressing common issues such as algae outbreaks, disease outbreaks, and coral pests promptly and effectively, aquarists can maintain a healthy and balanced reef aquarium ecosystem. Through careful observation, proactive management, and adherence to best practices, hobbyists can overcome challenges and create a thriving aquatic environment for their coral, fish, and invertebrate inhabitants to flourish.

Chapter 7

Lighting and Photosynthesis

Lighting plays a crucial role in the health, growth, and coloration of coral reefs and their inhabitants. In this chapter, we'll learn the fascinating relationship between lighting and photosynthesis in reef aquariums. From understanding the basics of light spectrum and intensity to optimizing lighting setups for coral health and growth, we'll delve into the intricate world of aquarium lighting and its impact on the vibrant ecosystems we create. Join me and unravel the mysteries of lighting and photosynthesis and learn how to harness the power of light to cultivate thriving reef aquariums.

Importance of Lighting in Reef Aquariums

Lighting is one of the most critical factors influencing the health and vitality of coral reefs and their inhabitants in a reef aquarium setting. And so here, we are going to know the multifaceted importance of lighting and its profound effects on photosynthesis, coral growth, and overall ecosystem stability.

Photosynthesis and Coral Symbiosis

Many corals, particularly those belonging to the Scleractinia order, have developed a symbiotic

117

relationship with photosynthetic algae known as zooxanthellae. These algae reside within coral tissues and harness light energy through photosynthesis, converting it into sugars that nourish both the algae and the coral host.

Light serves as the primary energy source for photosynthesis, providing the necessary photons for chlorophyll molecules within zooxanthellae to capture and convert light energy into chemical energy. This energy fuels the synthesis of sugars, which are essential for coral growth, reproduction, and calcification.

Coral Health and Growth

Different wavelengths of light have varying effects on coral health and growth. Photosynthetic pigments such as chlorophyll a, chlorophyll c2, and accessory pigments like carotenoids and xanthophylls absorb light at specific wavelengths, with red and blue light being particularly important for photosynthesis. Adequate light intensity is crucial for supporting photosynthesis and promoting healthy coral growth. Insufficient light can inhibit photosynthetic activity, leading to reduced growth, pale coloration, and increased susceptibility to stressors such as disease and predation.

The duration of light exposure, or photoperiod, influences coral metabolism, behavior, and reproduction. Mimicking natural light cycles, with a period of daylight followed by a period of darkness, helps regulate physiological processes and promote natural behaviors in reef aquarium inhabitants.

Coral Coloration and Pigment Regulation

Light spectrum and intensity play key roles in regulating the expression of pigments responsible for coral coloration. Vibrant colors in corals are attributed to the presence of fluorescent proteins, chromoproteins, and pigments such as chlorophyll, carotenoids, and phycobilins.

Some coral pigments act as photoprotective compounds, shielding coral tissues from excessive light exposure and harmful ultraviolet (UV) radiation. By absorbing and dissipating excess light energy, these pigments help mitigate oxidative stress and prevent photodamage to coral symbionts.

Ecosystem Stability and Biodiversity

Photosynthesis driven by light energy forms the foundation of primary productivity in coral reef ecosystems. Photosynthetic organisms, including corals, algae, and symbiotic zooxanthellae, convert inorganic carbon into organic matter, supporting a diverse array of marine life. The availability of light and photosynthetic productivity influence food chain dynamics and trophic interactions within reef ecosystems. Zooplankton, small fish, and invertebrates feed on organic matter produced through photosynthesis, serving as prey for higher trophic levels and contributing to ecosystem biodiversity.

Coral reefs provide essential habitat structure and shelter for numerous marine species, supporting a rich diversity of flora and fauna. Adequate light availability is crucial for sustaining coral reef ecosystems, as it directly influences coral growth rates, reef accretion, and the structural complexity of reef habitats.

In summary, lighting plays a pivotal role in the health, growth, and stability of reef aquarium ecosystems. By understanding the importance of light spectrum, intensity, and photoperiod in supporting photosynthesis, coral health, and ecosystem dynamics, aquarists can optimize lighting setups to create vibrant and sustainable reef aquariums teeming with life.

Types of Lighting Systems

Selecting the right lighting system is crucial for creating a thriving reef aquarium environment that supports the health and growth of corals and other photosynthetic organisms. In this section, we'll explore the various types of lighting systems commonly used in reef aquariums, discussing their features, benefits, and considerations for optimal performance.

Fluorescent Lighting

1. T5 Fluorescent Fixtures: T5 fluorescent fixtures are a popular choice among reef aquarists for their efficiency, versatility, and affordability. These fixtures use high-output T5 fluorescent tubes that produce intense light output while consuming relatively low energy. T5 bulbs come in various spectrums to accommodate different coral lighting requirements.

2. Compact Fluorescent (CF) Lighting: Compact fluorescent bulbs are smaller and more compact than traditional T5 tubes, making them suitable for smaller aquariums or supplemental lighting. CF bulbs offer a wide

range of color temperatures and spectrums, allowing aquarists to customize lighting for specific coral species or aesthetic preferences.

Metal Halide Lighting

Metal halide fixtures produce intense, penetrating light that closely mimics natural sunlight, making them ideal for deep aquariums or tanks with light-demanding corals. Metal halide bulbs emit a broad spectrum of light, including ultraviolet (UV) radiation, which can enhance coral coloration and growth.

Metal halide fixtures often feature adjustable reflectors or lenses that allow aquarists to focus and direct light onto specific areas of the aquarium. This flexibility enables precise control over light intensity and distribution, optimizing coverage for coral colonies and minimizing light spillage.

LED Lighting

Light-Emitting Diode (LED) Fixtures: LED lighting has revolutionized the reef aquarium hobby with its energy efficiency, customizable programming, and long lifespan. LED fixtures offer a wide range of color options, including full-spectrum lighting with adjustable intensity and color temperature settings.

Many LED fixtures come equipped with programmable controllers or software applications that allow users to create custom lighting schedules, simulate natural sunrise and sunset effects, and adjust color spectrum and intensity throughout the day. This level of customization enables aquarists to tailor lighting to the specific needs of their coral inhabitants.

Hybrid Lighting Systems

Hybrid lighting systems combine multiple lighting technologies, such as T5 fluorescent, metal halide, and LED lighting, into a single fixture. These systems offer the benefits of each lighting type, providing a versatile and customizable lighting solution for reef aquariums. By combining different lighting technologies, hybrid fixtures can produce a broader spectrum of light that closely resembles natural sunlight. This enhanced spectrum promotes coral health, coloration, and growth while minimizing shadowing and hot spots within the aquarium.

Considerations for Lighting Selection

1. Coral Requirements: Different coral species have varying lighting requirements, with some species preferring high-intensity lighting while others thrive under lower light levels. Consider the light preferences of your coral inhabitants

when selecting a lighting system and choose fixtures that can provide adequate light intensity and spectrum for their needs.

2. Aquarium Depth and Size: The depth and size of your aquarium influence the choice of lighting system, as deeper tanks may require higher-intensity lighting to penetrate to the bottom. Calculate the appropriate light coverage and intensity based on the dimensions of your aquarium to ensure uniform lighting distribution and sufficient PAR (Photosynthetically Active Radiation) levels throughout.

3. Energy Efficiency and Cost: Consider the energy efficiency and operating costs of different lighting systems, taking into account factors such as bulb lifespan, electricity consumption, and initial investment. LED lighting, while initially more expensive, may offer long-term savings in energy costs and bulb replacement compared to traditional fluorescent or metal halide fixtures.

4. Lighting Control and Programming: Evaluate the control features and programmability of lighting systems, as advanced control options can enhance flexibility and customization. Look for fixtures with user-friendly controllers or smartphone apps that allow you to adjust lighting parameters, create custom lighting schedules, and simulate natural lighting conditions.

In conclusion, choosing the right lighting system is essential for creating a healthy and visually stunning reef aquarium. Whether you opt for fluorescent, metal halide, LED, or hybrid lighting, consider the specific needs of your coral inhabitants, aquarium size, energy efficiency, and control options to select a lighting system that will support the growth and vibrancy of your aquatic ecosystem.

Lighting Requirements for Different Corals

Understanding the specific lighting requirements of different coral species is essential for providing optimal conditions for their growth, coloration, and overall health in a reef aquarium. In this section, we'll get to know the diverse lighting preferences of various coral types, from low-light soft corals to high-light SPS (Small Polyp Stony) corals, and provide guidance on selecting the right lighting system to meet their needs.

Low-Light Corals

1. Mushroom Corals (Corallimorphs): Mushroom corals are soft-bodied corals that thrive in low to moderate lighting conditions. They prefer subdued lighting with minimal intensity to prevent overexposure and maintain their characteristic round, disc-shaped morphology. LED fixtures with adjustable intensity settings are well-suited for providing gentle illumination without causing stress to mushroom corals.

2. Zoanthids and Palythoa: Zoanthids and Palythoa are colorful, colonial corals that can adapt to a wide range of lighting conditions,

from low to high intensity. While they can tolerate lower light levels, these corals exhibit more vibrant colors and faster growth under moderate to high light. T5 fluorescent or LED fixtures with a spectrum rich in blue and violet wavelengths enhance coloration and stimulate polyp extension in Zoanthids and Palythoa colonies.

Moderate-Light Corals

1. LPS Corals (Large Polyp Stony): LPS corals, including Torch corals, Hammer corals, and Brain corals, require moderate to high lighting levels to thrive. They possess large polyps and symbiotic zooxanthellae that benefit from intense light for photosynthesis. Metal halide or LED fixtures with a balanced spectrum of blue, white, and red wavelengths provide sufficient light penetration and intensity to support the growth and coloration of LPS corals.

2. Leather Corals: Leather corals, such as Toadstool corals and Finger corals, are soft corals that can tolerate a wide range of lighting

intensities. While they can adapt to low-light environments, they exhibit enhanced polyp extension and brighter coloration under moderate to high light. LED fixtures with adjustable intensity and spectrum control allow aquarists to customize lighting to meet the preferences of leather corals and promote their health and vitality.

High-Light Corals

1. SPS Corals (Small Polyp Stony): SPS corals, including Acropora, Montipora, and Pocillopora, are among the most light-demanding corals commonly kept in reef aquariums. They require intense, high-quality lighting to support rapid growth, vibrant coloration, and intricate skeletal formation. LED fixtures with high-output diodes and customizable spectrum and intensity settings are ideal for providing the precise lighting conditions needed to maintain healthy and thriving SPS coral colonies.

2. Clam Corals (Tridacna species): Tridacna species, also known as giant clams, are photosynthetic organisms that rely on

128

symbiotic algae for nutrition. These corals require intense, direct lighting to sustain their zooxanthellae populations and promote growth. Metal halide fixtures with high light output and broad spectrum coverage closely resemble natural sunlight and provide the intense illumination necessary for the health and vibrancy of clam corals.

Considerations for Lighting Placement and Acclimation

- Lighting Placement: Position lighting fixtures to ensure uniform coverage and appropriate light distribution throughout the aquarium. Use mounting brackets, suspension kits, or adjustable arms to adjust the height and angle of fixtures to suit the lighting preferences of different coral species and minimize shadowing and light spillage.

- Acclimation Period: When introducing corals to a new lighting environment or upgrading lighting fixtures, allow for a gradual acclimation period to prevent photodamage and stress.

Slowly increase light intensity and duration over several weeks, monitoring coral response and adjusting lighting settings as needed to ensure a smooth transition and minimize the risk of bleaching or tissue damage.

Understanding the lighting requirements of different coral species is essential for creating a balanced and sustainable reef aquarium ecosystem. By selecting the appropriate lighting system and providing optimal lighting conditions tailored to the needs of your corals, you can create a vibrant and visually stunning underwater landscape that promotes the health and vitality of your aquatic inhabitants.

Lighting Schedule and Spectrum

Developing a well-planned lighting schedule and selecting the appropriate spectrum are crucial aspects of reef aquarium husbandry, as they directly impact the health, growth, and coloration of coral inhabitants. In this section, we'll explore the factors to consider when designing a lighting schedule and choosing the optimal spectrum for your reef aquarium lighting system.

Lighting Schedule

Consistency in lighting schedules is key to maintaining a stable environment for reef aquarium inhabitants. Establish a regular photoperiod with consistent on/off times each day to mimic natural light cycles and provide a stable environment for photosynthetic organisms. When programming lighting schedules, incorporate gradual transitions between light and dark periods to mimic natural sunrise and sunset effects. This gradual transition helps reduce stress on aquarium inhabitants and allows them to acclimate to changes in light intensity gradually.

Create dawn and dusk effects by gradually increasing or decreasing light intensity and color temperature during the transition periods between day and night. This mimics the gradual changes in natural light conditions and encourages natural behaviors in aquarium inhabitants, such as feeding and spawning.

During the midday period, when the sun is at its highest point in the sky, provide the highest light intensity to simulate peak sunlight conditions. This peak intensity period promotes photosynthesis and provides sufficient energy for coral growth and metabolism.

Consider incorporating moonlight simulation into your lighting schedule to simulate lunar cycles and provide low-level illumination during the night. Moonlighting enhances nocturnal behaviors in fish and invertebrates while providing subtle ambient lighting for nighttime viewing.

Lighting Spectrum

The spectrum of light emitted by your lighting system influences coral health, growth, and coloration. Different wavelengths of light penetrate the water column to varying degrees, affecting the depth at which corals receive adequate light for photosynthesis. Aim for a full-spectrum lighting solution that provides a balanced combination of wavelengths, including blue, violet, green, yellow, orange, and red. Full-spectrum lighting closely resembles natural sunlight and ensures that corals receive the full range of light required for optimal photosynthesis and coloration.

Blue and violet wavelengths are particularly important for coral health and fluorescence. These wavelengths penetrate water effectively and stimulate chlorophyll and accessory pigment absorption, promoting photosynthesis and enhancing coral coloration and fluorescence.

While excessive UV radiation can be harmful to corals and other organisms, small amounts of UV light can promote natural fluorescence and coloration in certain coral species. LED fixtures with UV diodes can provide controlled UV supplementation without causing harm to coral symbionts. Choose lighting fixtures with adjustable spectrum control features that allow you to customize light color temperature and intensity to meet the specific requirements of your coral inhabitants. Adjustable spectrum control enables fine-tuning of lighting parameters to enhance coral coloration, growth, and overall aesthetic appeal.

Spectrum Considerations for Coral Health

- PAR (Photosynthetically Active Radiation): Consider the PAR output of your lighting system when selecting the spectrum for your reef aquarium. PAR measures the intensity of light within the spectral range (400-700 nm) that is utilized by photosynthetic organisms for photosynthesis. Aim for a balanced spectrum that provides sufficient PAR levels to support coral growth and photosynthesis.

- Color Rendering Index (CRI): The Color Rendering Index measures the ability of a light source to accurately render colors compared to natural sunlight. Choose lighting fixtures with a high CRI rating to ensure that coral colors appear vibrant and true to their natural appearance under artificial lighting.

- Spectral Distribution: Evaluate the spectral distribution of your lighting system to ensure that it provides adequate coverage across the entire visible light spectrum. Balancing blue, violet, and white wavelengths ensures that corals receive the full spectrum of light required for photosynthesis and pigment synthesis.

- Photosynthetic Efficiency: Different coral species have varying photosynthetic efficiency and light requirements. Research the lighting preferences of your coral inhabitants and select a lighting spectrum that closely matches their natural habitat conditions to promote optimal health, growth, and coloration.

In summary, designing a lighting schedule and selecting the appropriate spectrum are critical components of reef aquarium management. By establishing a consistent lighting schedule that mimics natural light cycles and choosing a balanced spectrum that provides sufficient PAR levels and promotes coral health and coloration, aquarists can create an optimal lighting environment for their reef aquarium inhabitants to thrive and flourish.

Chapter 8

Coral Reef Ecosystems

Coral reefs are among the most biodiverse and ecologically important ecosystems on the planet, teeming with a mesmerizing array of marine life and supporting millions of species. In this chapter, we'll embark on a journey to knowledge about the fascinating world of coral reef ecosystems. From the vibrant coral communities to the myriad of fish, invertebrates, and algae that inhabit these underwater realms, we'll get to see the interconnected relationships, ecological dynamics, and conservation challenges facing coral reefs today. Join us as we unravel the mysteries and marvels of coral reef ecosystems and discover the beauty and complexity of these underwater wonders.

Understanding Coral Biology

Coral reefs are intricate ecosystems built by millions of tiny organisms known as coral polyps. In this section, we'll gain insights into the fascinating world of coral biology, exploring the anatomy, physiology, and life cycle of these remarkable creatures. By gaining a deeper understanding of coral biology, we can appreciate the critical role corals play in reef ecosystems and the challenges they face in today's changing world.

Anatomy of Coral Polyps

Coral polyps are small, cylindrical animals with a tubular body and a mouth surrounded by tentacles. The polyp's body is protected by a calcium carbonate skeleton secreted by specialized cells called calicoblasts, forming the characteristic reef-building structures we recognize as coral colonies. The tentacles of coral polyps contain stinging cells called nematocysts, which are used for prey capture and defense. The mouth serves as both an entrance for food and an outlet for waste, allowing polyps to efficiently feed and expel metabolic byproducts.

Coral Reproduction and Life Cycle

Corals reproduce asexually through budding, fragmentation, and basal plate division. Budding involves the formation of new polyps from existing ones, while fragmentation occurs when coral colonies break apart, with each fragment developing into a new colony. Basal plate division involves the division of a colony into multiple segments, each capable of forming a new colony.

Corals also reproduce sexually through the release of gametes into the water during mass spawning events. Synchronous spawning occurs when corals release eggs and sperm simultaneously, leading to the fertilization and development of coral larvae known as planulae. Planulae drift with ocean currents before settling on suitable substrate to begin the process of colony formation.

Symbiotic Relationship with Zooxanthellae

Many coral species form a symbiotic relationship with single-celled algae called zooxanthellae, which live within coral tissues and provide corals with energy through photosynthesis. In return, corals provide zooxanthellae with shelter and nutrients. This mutualistic relationship is essential for coral health and productivity, as zooxanthellae contribute a significant portion of the energy corals need to survive and grow.

Photosynthesis by zooxanthellae generates sugars and oxygen, which fuel coral metabolism and calcification. The byproducts of photosynthesis, including glucose and oxygen, are transferred to coral tissues, where they are used for respiration, growth, and reproduction. Corals rely on photosynthesis for up to 90% of their energy requirements, highlighting the importance of the symbiotic relationship with zooxanthellae.

Coral Feeding and Nutrition

While corals primarily rely on photosynthesis for energy, they also engage in suspension feeding to capture plankton and organic particles from the water column. Coral tentacles contain specialized cells called cnidocytes, which release nematocysts to immobilize prey. Once captured, prey items are transferred to the mouth for ingestion and digestion. Corals can also absorb dissolved organic matter and nutrients directly from seawater through their tissues. This facultative feeding strategy allows corals to supplement their nutritional needs during periods of low prey availability or reduced photosynthetic activity.

So, by understanding the biology of coral polyps, their reproductive strategies, symbiotic relationships with zooxanthellae, and feeding behaviors, we gain a deeper appreciation for the remarkable adaptability and resilience of these vital reef-building organisms. Understanding coral biology is key to conserving and preserving coral reef ecosystems for future generations to enjoy and appreciate.

Symbiotic Relationships in the Reef

Coral reefs are bustling ecosystems where a multitude of organisms form intricate and interconnected relationships to survive and thrive. Here, we will look into the fascinating world of symbiosis in the reef, where various organisms engage in mutually beneficial interactions that shape the health and diversity of these underwater communities. From coral-algae partnerships to fish-cleaning stations, symbiotic relationships play a vital role in maintaining the balance and resilience of coral reef ecosystems.

Coral-Algae Symbiosis

- Zooxanthellae and Corals: One of the most well-known symbiotic relationships in coral reefs is the partnership between corals and zooxanthellae, single-celled algae that reside within coral tissues. Zooxanthellae harness sunlight through photosynthesis, producing sugars and oxygen that fuel coral metabolism and calcification. In return, corals provide zooxanthellae with shelter and nutrients, creating a mutually beneficial relationship essential for coral reef health and productivity.

Coral-algae symbiosis provides corals with up to 90% of their energy needs, allowing them to thrive in

142

nutrient-poor tropical waters. The sugars produced by zooxanthellae fuel coral growth, reproduction, and resilience to environmental stressors such as temperature fluctuations and sedimentation. Additionally, the vibrant colors of coral colonies are attributed to pigments and fluorescent proteins produced by zooxanthellae, enhancing the visual beauty of coral reefs.

Fish Cleaning Stations

Fish cleaning stations are areas within the reef where small cleaner fish, such as cleaner wrasses and cleaner shrimp, provide cleaning services to larger reef fish by removing parasites, dead skin, and algae from their bodies. In exchange for their services, cleaner fish receive a nutritious meal and protection from predators.

Cleaner fish attract clients by performing distinctive cleaning behaviors, such as displaying vibrant colors and performing characteristic swimming patterns. Larger fish visit cleaning stations regularly to benefit from the cleaning services provided by cleaner fish, forming mutualistic relationships that benefit both parties.

Coral-Feeding Relationships

Coral polyps engage in suspension feeding to capture plankton and organic particles from the water column. The tentacles of coral polyps contain specialized cells called cnidocytes, which release stinging cells called nematocysts to immobilize prey. Once captured, prey items are transferred to the mouth for ingestion and digestion.

Various reef inhabitants, including fish, crustaceans, and mollusks, rely on corals as a food source or shelter. For example, butterflyfish and angelfish feed on coral polyps, while certain species of shrimp and crabs seek refuge within coral branches. These relationships, while not always mutually beneficial, contribute to the complex food web and trophic dynamics of coral reef ecosystems.

Coral-Microbial Symbiosis

Coral reefs harbor diverse microbial communities that play critical roles in nutrient cycling, disease resistance, and coral health. Beneficial bacteria residing within coral tissues help regulate nutrient availability, detoxify harmful compounds, and protect corals from pathogenic microbes.

Imbalances in microbial communities, known as dysbiosis, can contribute to coral disease outbreaks and declines in reef health. Environmental stressors such as pollution, overfishing, and climate change can disrupt microbial symbioses within corals, leading to increased susceptibility to disease and bleaching events.

Symbiotic relationships are fundamental to the functioning and resilience of coral reef ecosystems, fostering cooperation and mutual dependence among diverse organisms. By understanding and appreciating the intricate web of symbiotic interactions in the reef, we gain insights into the complex dynamics and interconnectedness of these biodiverse underwater communities.

Importance of Biodiversity

Biodiversity is the cornerstone of coral reef ecosystems, contributing to their resilience, productivity, and ecological function. There are myriad of benefits of biodiversity in coral reefs, from supporting ecosystem stability to providing essential services for human well-being. By understanding the importance of biodiversity, we can appreciate the critical role it plays in sustaining healthy and vibrant coral reef ecosystems.

Ecosystem Stability and Resilience

Biodiversity in coral reefs fosters complex networks of species interactions, including predation, competition, and mutualism, which contribute to ecosystem stability and resilience. Diverse species assemblages provide redundant ecological functions and buffers against environmental fluctuations, helping coral reefs withstand disturbances such as storms, disease outbreaks, and climate change. High levels of biodiversity enhance the resilience of coral reef ecosystems by increasing their capacity to adapt to changing environmental conditions. Species diversity promotes genetic diversity within populations, enabling organisms to evolve and acclimate to new environmental stressors over time. Resilient ecosystems with diverse species assemblages

146

are better equipped to recover from disturbances and maintain ecological integrity in the face of ongoing environmental change.

Nutrient Cycling and Productivity

Biodiversity in coral reefs contributes to the efficient cycling of nutrients through various ecological processes, including photosynthesis, respiration, and decomposition. Microbial communities, algae, and filter-feeding organisms play critical roles in nutrient recycling, converting organic matter into forms that can be utilized by primary producers such as corals and algae. Biodiversity enhances primary productivity in coral reef ecosystems by supporting a diverse array of primary producers, including corals, algae, and seagrasses. High levels of primary productivity fuel food webs and support diverse communities of herbivores, carnivores, and omnivores, contributing to the overall productivity and biomass of coral reef ecosystems.

Ecological Services and Human Well-being

Coral reefs support valuable fisheries resources that provide food, income, and livelihoods for millions of people worldwide. Diverse fish assemblages, including commercially important species such as grouper, snapper, and tuna, contribute to global food security and economic prosperity in coastal communities dependent on reef-based fisheries.

Biodiversity in coral reefs attracts millions of tourists and recreational divers each year, generating revenue and supporting local economies through ecotourism and dive tourism activities. Vibrant coral reefs teeming with diverse marine life offer unparalleled opportunities for snorkeling, diving, and underwater photography, enriching the lives of visitors and fostering appreciation for marine biodiversity.

Scientific and Educational Value

Coral reefs are hotspots of scientific discovery and research, offering invaluable opportunities to study complex ecological processes, species interactions, and ecosystem dynamics. Biodiversity in coral reefs provides a wealth of research subjects for scientists studying topics ranging from marine biology and ecology to climate change and conservation biology. They serve as living classrooms and educational resources for students, educators, and the general public, offering opportunities to learn about marine biodiversity, ecosystem function, and conservation challenges. Dive centers, marine parks, and educational institutions provide immersive experiences and educational programs that raise awareness about the importance of biodiversity conservation and stewardship of coral reef ecosystems.

Biodiversity is essential for the health, resilience, and sustainability of coral reef ecosystems. By preserving and protecting biodiversity in coral reefs, we can safeguard the myriad benefits they provide, from supporting ecosystem stability and productivity to enhancing human well-being and fostering scientific discovery. Investing in biodiversity conservation efforts is essential for ensuring the long-term health and viability of coral reef ecosystems for future generations to enjoy and appreciate.

Coral Conservation Efforts

Coral reefs face unprecedented threats from human activities, including climate change, overfishing, pollution, and habitat destruction. There are diverse range of conservation efforts aimed at protecting and preserving coral reefs worldwide. From marine protected areas to community-based initiatives, these conservation efforts play a crucial role in safeguarding the future of coral reef ecosystems and the countless species that depend on them for survival.

Marine Protected Areas (MPAs)

Marine protected areas are designated areas of oceanic or coastal waters that are managed to conserve marine ecosystems and biodiversity. MPAs can include coral reefs, seagrass beds, mangroves, and other critical habitats. By restricting or regulating human activities such as fishing, diving, and coastal development, MPAs help reduce pressures on coral reef ecosystems and promote recovery of degraded habitats.

MPAs provide numerous benefits for coral reef conservation, including protecting biodiversity, maintaining fish stocks, and supporting ecosystem resilience. Well-managed MPAs can enhance coral reef health, increase fish biomass, and promote the recovery of degraded habitats. They also serve as valuable research sites and educational resources for scientists, educators, and the general public.

Coral Reef Restoration

Coral reef restoration involves the propagation and transplantation of coral fragments or larvae onto degraded reefs to promote reef recovery and resilience. Techniques such as coral farming, coral gardening, and larval rearing are used to propagate corals in nurseries before transplanting them onto damaged or degraded reefs. Restoration efforts aim to enhance coral cover, diversity, and ecosystem function in areas affected by coral bleaching, disease, or other disturbances.

In addition to natural coral transplantation, artificial reef structures such as coral frames, concrete modules, and reef balls are deployed to create habitat for corals and other reef organisms. These structures mimic natural reef substrate and provide attachment sites for coral larvae, enhancing recruitment and colonization on degraded reefs.

Community-Based Conservation

Community-based conservation initiatives involve collaborating with local communities to develop and implement sustainable management strategies for coral reef resources. By engaging stakeholders in decision-making processes and empowering local communities to manage their natural resources, community-based conservation efforts promote social equity, cultural resilience, and environmental stewardship. Indigenous and traditional communities possess valuable ecological knowledge and practices that have sustained coral reef ecosystems for generations. Community-based conservation initiatives recognize the importance of traditional ecological knowledge and seek to integrate indigenous perspectives and practices into modern conservation strategies, enhancing the effectiveness and sustainability of conservation efforts.

Climate Change Mitigation and Adaptation

Climate change poses one of the greatest threats to coral reef ecosystems, leading to rising sea temperatures, ocean acidification, and more frequent and severe coral bleaching events. Conservation efforts to mitigate climate change include reducing carbon emissions through energy efficiency measures, transitioning to renewable energy sources, and advocating for policies to limit global warming.

In addition to mitigating climate change, conservation efforts focus on enhancing the resilience of coral reef ecosystems to climate-related stressors. Strategies such as coral reef management, water quality improvement, and habitat restoration aim to increase reef resilience and adaptive capacity, allowing corals and other reef organisms to withstand and recover from environmental disturbances.

In conclusion, coral conservation efforts encompass a wide range of strategies and approaches aimed at protecting and preserving coral reef ecosystems for future generations. By implementing marine protected areas, conducting coral reef restoration, engaging local communities, and addressing climate change, we can work together to safeguard the biodiversity, resilience, and ecological integrity of coral reefs worldwide. Through collaborative action and collective stewardship, we can ensure that coral reefs continue to thrive as vibrant and biodiverse ecosystems for generations to come.

Chapter 9

Advanced Topics and Techniques

In this chapter, we move into advanced topics and techniques for reef aquarium enthusiasts who are looking to expand their knowledge and skills in coral reef husbandry. From specialized aquascaping techniques to advanced water chemistry management, we'll explore the intricacies of maintaining a thriving reef aquarium ecosystem. Whether you're a seasoned aquarist seeking to enhance your expertise or a newcomer eager to venture into the complexities of reefkeeping, this chapter offers valuable insights and guidance to take your reef aquarium hobby to the next level. Join along, as we explore the cutting-edge of reef aquarium science and technology, unlocking new possibilities for creating and maintaining stunning coral reef ecosystems.

Advanced Filtration Methods

Filtration is a crucial aspect of reef aquarium husbandry, responsible for maintaining water quality and creating a healthy environment for coral reef inhabitants. There are advanced filtration methods and technologies that go beyond traditional filtration systems, offering enhanced efficiency, versatility, and performance. From protein skimmers to fluidized bed reactors, these advanced filtration methods provide aquarists with innovative solutions for achieving optimal water quality and supporting the health and vitality of coral reef ecosystems.

Protein Skimmers

Protein skimmers, also known as foam fractionators, are mechanical filtration devices that remove dissolved organic compounds and other contaminants from aquarium water through a process called foam fractionation. Water is injected into a column or chamber containing a rising column of fine air bubbles, which attract and capture organic molecules and particulate matter. The resulting foam, rich in organic waste, is then collected and removed from the system, effectively reducing nutrient levels and improving water quality.

Protein skimmers come in various configurations, including in-sump, hang-on-back, and external models. In-sump protein skimmers are installed directly in the aquarium sump or filtration chamber, while hang-on-back models hang on the back of the aquarium and draw water through an intake tube. External protein skimmers are installed outside the aquarium system and connected to a separate pump for water circulation.

Advanced protein skimmers may incorporate additional features such as adjustable water flow rates, variable foam height control, and automatic waste collection mechanisms. These features allow aquarists to fine-tune skimmer performance and optimize nutrient removal based on specific aquarium requirements and livestock needs.

Fluidized Bed Reactors (FBRs)

Fluidized bed reactors (FBRs) are filtration devices that utilize a suspended bed of inert media particles to promote biological filtration and nutrient export. Water is pumped into the reactor, creating a turbulent flow that suspends the media particles and creates a fluidized bed. Beneficial bacteria colonize the media surface, where they metabolize organic waste and convert harmful compounds such as ammonia and nitrite into less toxic forms.

FBRs can be filled with various types of media, including biopellets, bio balls, and porous ceramic rings, depending on the specific filtration requirements and goals of the aquarist. Biopellets, for example, provide a carbon source for denitrifying bacteria, while porous ceramic media offer a large surface area for bacterial colonization and nutrient processing.

FBRs can be integrated into existing filtration systems, such as sumps or external filtration units, to complement other filtration methods such as protein skimming and mechanical filtration. By incorporating FBRs into the filtration system, aquarists can enhance nutrient export and maintain stable water quality parameters in the aquarium.

Refugiums and Algae Turf Scrubbers (ATS)

Refugiums are separate compartments or chambers connected to the main aquarium system, designed to provide a sanctuary for beneficial microorganisms, macroalgae, and small invertebrates. Refugiums enhance biological filtration by promoting the growth of microorganisms that consume organic waste and excess nutrients, such as nitrates and phosphates. Macroalgae species such as Chaetomorpha and Caulerpa are commonly cultivated in refugiums to absorb nutrients and improve water quality.

Algae turf scrubbers (ATS) are filtration devices that utilize actively growing algae to remove excess nutrients from aquarium water. Water is passed over a screen or mesh surface covered with algae, where photosynthesis occurs and algae absorb nutrients such as nitrates and phosphates. The algae biomass can then be harvested and removed from the system, effectively exporting nutrients and reducing the risk of algae overgrowth in the main aquarium.

Calcium Reactors and Kalkwasser Reactors

Calcium reactors are specialized filtration devices used to maintain stable calcium and alkalinity levels in reef aquariums, essential for supporting coral growth and calcification. The reactor chamber is filled with calcium carbonate media, such as aragonite or crushed coral, which dissolves in acidic water to release calcium and carbonate ions. By controlling the flow rate and CO_2 injection, aquarists can regulate the dissolution rate of the media and adjust calcium and alkalinity levels to meet the demands of corals and other calcifying organisms.

Kalkwasser reactors, also known as limewater reactors, utilize a solution of calcium hydroxide (kalkwasser) to supplement calcium and alkalinity levels in reef aquariums. A kalkwasser solution is prepared and dosed into the aquarium system using a dosing pump or gravity-fed dripper. Kalkwasser reacts with carbon dioxide in the water to form calcium carbonate precipitate, which is then removed via protein skimming or mechanical filtration. Kalkwasser dosing helps maintain calcium and alkalinity balance in reef aquariums and promotes coral health and growth.

Monitoring and Automation

Advanced filtration systems often incorporate monitoring devices such as probes, sensors, and controllers to monitor key water quality parameters, including temperature, pH, salinity, and nutrient levels. These monitoring devices provide real-time data on aquarium conditions, allowing aquarists to detect and respond to changes in water quality promptly.

Automation systems and controllers can be used to automate filtration processes, such as protein skimming, water changes, and dosing of additives and supplements. By programming customized schedules and settings, aquarists can optimize filtration performance, maintain stable water parameters, and reduce the time and effort required for routine maintenance tasks.

Advanced filtration methods offer innovative solutions for maintaining optimal water quality and supporting the health and vitality of coral reef ecosystems. By incorporating protein skimmers, fluidized bed reactors, refugiums, calcium reactors, and other advanced filtration technologies into reef aquarium systems, aquarists can create stable and thriving aquatic environments conducive to the growth and well-being of corals and other reef inhabitants. Through careful selection, implementation, and maintenance of advanced filtration systems, aquarists can achieve their goals of creating stunning and sustainable reef aquariums for years to come.

Reef Chemistry and Additives

Maintaining proper water chemistry is essential for the health and vitality of coral reef ecosystems in aquariums. In this section, Let's gain more insight on reef chemistry, exploring the roles of key parameters such as calcium, alkalinity, and magnesium, as well as the use of additives to maintain optimal water quality. By understanding reef chemistry and utilizing appropriate additives, aquarists can create stable and thriving environments that support the growth and well-being of corals and other reef inhabitants.

Major Reef Chemistry Parameters

1. Calcium (Ca): Calcium is a critical element for coral skeletal growth and calcification. Corals extract calcium ions from seawater to form calcium carbonate skeletons, which provide structure and support for coral colonies. Maintaining stable calcium levels (typically 400-450 ppm) is essential for promoting coral growth and preventing skeletal dissolution.

2. Alkalinity (KH): Alkalinity, also known as carbonate hardness, is a measure of the buffering capacity of seawater against changes in pH. Alkalinity plays a vital role in stabilizing

162

pH levels and supporting coral calcification. Keeping alkalinity levels within the appropriate range (typically 8-12 dKH) ensures that corals have an adequate supply of carbonate ions for skeletal growth and maintenance.

3. Magnesium (Mg): Magnesium is an essential component of seawater chemistry, influencing the precipitation and dissolution of calcium carbonate. Maintaining stable magnesium levels (typically 1200-1350 ppm) helps prevent the formation of insoluble calcium carbonate precipitates and promotes coral calcification.

4. pH: pH is a measure of the acidity or alkalinity of seawater. Maintaining stable pH levels (typically 8.1-8.4) is crucial for supporting coral health and metabolic processes. Fluctuations in pH can stress corals and disrupt biological processes such as calcification and photosynthesis.

Reef Chemistry Additives

1. Calcium Supplements: Calcium supplements, such as calcium chloride and calcium carbonate, are used to replenish calcium levels in reef aquariums. These additives are dosed regularly to maintain stable calcium concentrations and promote coral growth and calcification. Calcium supplements should be used in conjunction with alkalinity supplements to maintain proper ion balance and prevent precipitation of calcium carbonate.

2. Alkalinity Supplements: Alkalinity supplements, such as sodium bicarbonate (baking soda) and sodium carbonate (soda ash), are used to maintain stable alkalinity levels in reef aquariums. These additives provide a source of carbonate ions for coral calcification and help stabilize pH levels. Alkalinity supplements should be dosed regularly to maintain consistent alkalinity concentrations and support coral health.

3. Magnesium Supplements: Magnesium supplements, such as magnesium chloride and

magnesium sulfate, are used to replenish magnesium levels in reef aquariums. These additives help maintain proper magnesium concentrations and prevent calcium carbonate precipitation. Magnesium supplements should be dosed as needed to maintain stable magnesium levels within the recommended range.

4. Trace Element Supplements: Trace element supplements, such as iodine, strontium, and potassium, are used to replenish essential trace elements that are depleted over time in reef aquariums. These additives support various biological processes, including coral growth, coloration, and metabolic functions. Trace element supplements should be dosed carefully according to manufacturer recommendations to avoid overdosing and potential negative effects on water quality.

Advanced Chemistry Monitoring and Control

Advanced water testing kits, including titration-based test kits and digital monitoring devices, are available to measure reef chemistry parameters with high accuracy and precision. These testing kits allow aquarists to monitor calcium, alkalinity, magnesium, and pH levels regularly and adjust supplementation accordingly to maintain optimal water quality.

Automated dosing systems can be used to precisely control the dosing of reef chemistry additives based on real-time water parameter measurements. These systems utilize dosing pumps and controllers to deliver precise doses of calcium, alkalinity, magnesium, and trace element supplements according to programmed schedules and setpoints. Automated dosing systems provide convenience and accuracy in maintaining stable reef chemistry parameters and supporting coral health.

Another one is pH controllers, pH controllers are devices that monitor and regulate pH levels in reef aquariums by controlling the dosing of alkalinity supplements or carbon dioxide (CO_2) injection. pH controllers help maintain stable pH levels within the desired range and prevent fluctuations that can stress corals and other reef inhabitants. By integrating pH controllers into the aquarium system, aquarists can

166

ensure optimal water chemistry conditions for coral growth and vitality.

Reef chemistry and additives play a crucial role in maintaining optimal water quality and supporting the health and growth of corals and other reef inhabitants in aquariums. By understanding the roles of key parameters such as calcium, alkalinity, and magnesium, and utilizing appropriate additives and monitoring techniques, aquarists can create stable and thriving reef environments that mimic natural coral reef ecosystems. Through careful management and supplementation of reef chemistry, aquarists can provide the conditions necessary for the long-term success and sustainability of their reef aquariums.

Propagating Corals

Coral propagation, also known as coral farming or coral aquaculture, is a vital practice in reef aquarium husbandry aimed at sustainably sourcing corals for the aquarium trade while reducing pressure on wild populations. There are fascinating process of propagating corals, from selecting parent colonies to fragging techniques and coral husbandry practices. By propagating corals responsibly, aquarists can contribute to coral conservation efforts and support the long-term health and sustainability of coral reef ecosystems.

Selecting Parent Colonies

When selecting parent colonies for coral propagation, it's essential to choose healthy, robust specimens with vibrant colors and good tissue integrity. Healthy corals are more likely to produce viable offspring and exhibit strong growth and resistance to stressors.

Maintaining genetic diversity is crucial for the long-term health and resilience of coral populations. Aquarists should select parent colonies from diverse genetic backgrounds to promote genetic variability and reduce the risk of inbreeding depression. Consideration should be given to the compatibility of parent colonies, particularly when propagating multiple coral species in the same aquarium. Avoid

168

placing aggressive or territorial species in close proximity to prevent competition and territorial disputes.

Fragging Techniques

To frag corals, aquarists will need specialized tools and equipment, including bone cutters, fragging shears, scalpels, and frag plugs or discs. It's essential to use clean and sterile tools to minimize the risk of introducing pathogens or contaminants to the coral fragments. There are several techniques for fragging corals, including cutting, breaking, and sawing. The chosen method will depend on the coral species, colony size, and fragging goals. Care should be taken to minimize stress and damage to the parent colony and ensure the production of viable fragments.

Fragments should be handled with care to avoid tissue damage and desiccation. Fragments can be placed on frag plugs or discs using reef-safe glue or epoxy to secure them in place. Fragments should be positioned upright and allowed to heal and encrust before being transferred to the main aquarium or coral propagation system.

Coral Husbandry Practices

1. Water Quality and Lighting: Maintaining stable water quality parameters, including temperature, salinity, pH, and nutrient levels, is essential for the health and growth of propagated corals. Adequate lighting is also crucial for photosynthesis and coral growth, with different coral species having varying light requirements.

2. Feeding and Nutrition: While corals obtain the majority of their nutritional requirements through photosynthesis, supplemental feeding can help support growth and coloration, particularly for fast-growing or nutrient-demanding species. Feeding small particles of phytoplankton or coral-specific planktonic foods can provide additional nutrients for coral health and vitality.

3. Pest and Disease Management: Regular monitoring for pests and diseases is essential to prevent outbreaks and maintain the health of propagated corals. Quarantine procedures should be implemented for new coral additions

170

to the aquarium to prevent the introduction of pests or pathogens to established colonies.

Conservation and Sustainability

Coral propagation plays a crucial role in reducing pressure on wild coral populations by providing a sustainable source of corals for the aquarium trade. By sourcing propagated corals from responsible aquaculture facilities, aquarists can support coral conservation efforts and minimize the impact on fragile reef ecosystems. Coral propagation is also used in coral restoration initiatives aimed at rehabilitating degraded reef habitats and promoting reef resilience. Propagated corals can be used to establish new coral colonies in damaged areas, enhance genetic diversity, and restore ecosystem function.

Educating aquarists and the general public about the importance of coral propagation and sustainable reef aquarium practices is essential for promoting conservation awareness and fostering stewardship of coral reef ecosystems. Outreach programs, workshops, and online resources can help raise awareness about coral conservation and inspire action to protect these invaluable marine resources.

Coral propagation is a valuable practice in reef aquarium husbandry that offers numerous benefits for coral conservation and sustainability. By selecting suitable parent colonies, employing fragging techniques, practicing proper coral husbandry, and supporting conservation initiatives, aquarists can play a vital role in preserving coral reef ecosystems for future generations to enjoy and appreciate. Through responsible propagation and stewardship, we can ensure the continued health and vitality of coral reefs in aquariums and in the wild.

Breeding Marine Fish

Breeding marine fish in captivity is a challenging yet rewarding endeavor that contributes to the sustainability of the aquarium trade and reduces pressure on wild fish populations. In this section, we will gain some knowledge on marine fish breeding, from selecting breeding pairs to raising fry and overcoming common challenges. By understanding the principles of fish reproduction and implementing effective breeding techniques, aquarists can play a vital role in conserving marine fish species and promoting responsible aquarium husbandry.

Selecting Breeding Pairs

Choose fish species that are known to breed readily in captivity and are suitable for the size and setup of your aquarium. Some species, such as clownfish (Amphiprion spp.) and gobies (Gobiidae), are popular choices for beginner breeders due to their relatively straightforward breeding requirements and parental care behaviors.

Pair compatible individuals based on species, size, and temperament to minimize aggression and ensure successful spawning. Introduce potential breeding pairs to each other gradually and observe their behavior to ensure compatibility before attempting to breed them. Condition breeding pairs with a nutritious and varied diet rich in protein and vitamins to enhance reproductive readiness and egg quality. Ensure that breeding pairs are in optimal health and free from parasites or diseases before initiating spawning attempts.

Spawning and Egg Care

Create environmental cues, such as changes in temperature, photoperiod, or water quality, to simulate natural spawning conditions and trigger reproductive behaviors in breeding pairs. Some species may require specific triggers, such as lunar cycles or seasonal changes, to initiate spawning.

Monitor breeding pairs closely for signs of spawning behavior, such as courtship displays or nest preparation. Once eggs are laid, carefully collect them and transfer them to a separate rearing tank or container to prevent predation and ensure optimal conditions for egg development. Provide appropriate water flow, temperature, and lighting conditions for egg incubation and development. Monitor water quality parameters closely and perform regular water changes to maintain optimal conditions for egg hatching and fry survival.

Larval Rearing and Fry Care

1. Feeding Larvae: Offer appropriate live or enriched foods to larval fish to support growth and development during the early stages of life. Live rotifers, copepods, and newly hatched brine shrimp (Artemia) are commonly used as first foods for marine fish larvae due to their small size and nutritional value.

2. Tank Setup: Set up larval rearing tanks with appropriate filtration, aeration, and lighting to create a stable and healthy environment for fry growth. Provide hiding places and structure for fry to seek shelter and reduce stress.

3. Water Quality Management: Monitor water quality parameters closely and maintain stable water conditions throughout the larval rearing process. Perform regular water changes, maintain proper temperature and salinity levels, and ensure adequate oxygenation to support fry health and vitality.

Challenges and Considerations

- Disease Prevention: Implement strict hygiene protocols and quarantine procedures to prevent the introduction and spread of diseases in breeding and rearing facilities. Regular health checks and observation of fry behavior can help detect and treat diseases early to minimize losses.

- Nutritional Requirements: Research the nutritional requirements of larval fish species and provide a diverse and balanced diet to meet their specific needs. Experiment with different types of live and prepared foods to determine the most suitable diet for optimal growth and development.

- Rearing Techniques: Experiment with different rearing techniques, such as batch rearing or continuous flow systems, to optimize fry survival and growth rates. Monitor fry behavior and growth closely and adjust rearing protocols as needed to address any challenges or issues that arise.

Conservation and Sustainability

Breeding marine fish in captivity helps reduce the demand for wild-caught specimens and supports sustainable practices in the aquarium trade. By sourcing captive-bred fish, aquarists can contribute to conservation efforts and promote responsible stewardship of marine resources. Breeding endangered or threatened species in captivity can help preserve genetic diversity and prevent the extinction of vulnerable populations. Conservation breeding programs for rare or endangered species play a crucial role in species recovery and reintroduction efforts.

Educating aquarists and the general public about the importance of captive breeding and sustainable aquarium practices is essential for promoting conservation awareness and fostering support for conservation initiatives. Outreach programs, workshops, and educational resources can help raise awareness about marine fish breeding and inspire action to protect marine biodiversity.

Breeding marine fish in captivity offers numerous benefits for conservation, sustainability, and responsible aquarium husbandry. By selecting suitable breeding pairs, providing optimal spawning and rearing conditions, and addressing common challenges, aquarists can contribute to the conservation of marine fish species and promote the long-term health and viability of marine ecosystems. Through responsible breeding practices and conservation efforts, we can ensure a sustainable future for marine fish populations and the aquarium hobby as a whole.

Conclusion

Reefkeeping is not just a hobby; it's a journey of discovery, stewardship, and appreciation for the wonders of the ocean. Throughout this guide, we've explored the ins and outs of reef aquariums, from their captivating beauty to the balance of life within. As you embark on your reef aquarium journey, remember that each step you take is an opportunity to learn, grow, and contribute to the preservation of coral reef ecosystems.

Reefkeeping is a rewarding and fulfilling pursuit, offering endless opportunities for creativity, exploration, and connection with the natural world. As you delve into the depths of your aquarium, you'll witness the vibrant colors, patterns, and fascinating behaviors of coral reef inhabitants, reminding you of the incredible diversity and beauty of marine life.

Embrace the rewards of reefkeeping—the joy of witnessing coral growth, the satisfaction of creating a thriving ecosystem, and the sense of pride in knowing that you're making a positive impact on marine conservation. Whether you're a beginner or seasoned aquarist, every effort you make to care for your reef aquarium contributes to the greater goal of preserving coral reefs for future generations to enjoy.

As you embark on your reef aquarium journey, may you find inspiration in the beauty of the underwater world, strength in the challenges you face, and fulfillment in the bonds you form with your aquatic companions. Best wishes for a successful and rewarding reefkeeping experience, filled with wonder, discovery, and endless possibilities. Remember, your reef aquarium journey is not just about creating a beautiful display—it's about fostering a deeper connection with nature and becoming a steward of the ocean's treasures. Happy reefkeeping!

Made in United States
Troutdale, OR
04/28/2024

19504865R10106